D1431240

Timothy Findley

Twayne's World Author Series
Canadian Literature

Robert Lecker, Editor
McGill University

TWAS 875

TIMOTHY FINDLEY
Jerry Bauer

Timothy Findley

Diana Brydon

University of Guelph

Twayne Publishers
An Imprint of Simon & Schuster Macmillan
New York

Prentice Hall International
London • Mexico City • New Delhi • Singapore • Sydney • Toronto

Twayne's World Authors Series No. 875

Timothy Findley
Diana Brydon

Twayne Publishers
An Imprint of Simon & Schuster Macmillan
1633 Broadway
New York, NY 10019

Library of Congress Cataloging-in-Publication Data

Brydon, Diana.
    Timothy Findley / Diana Brydon.
        p.   cm. — (Twayne's world authors series ; TWAS 875. Canadian literature)
    Includes bibliographical references and index.
    ISBN 0-8057-1666-1 (alk. paper)
        1. Findley, Timothy—Criticism and interpretation.   I. Title.
II. Series: Twayne's world authors series ; TWAS 875.   III. Series:
Twayne's world authors series.   Canadian literature.
PR9199.3.F52Z58   1998
818'5409—dc21   98-29217
                                                           CIP

This paper meets the requirements of ANSI/NISO Z3948-1992 (Permanence of Paper).

10 9 8 7 6 5 4 3 2 1

Printed in the United States of America

Contents

Preface

This book introduces new readers to the pleasures and challenges of reading Timothy Findley's work, while leading those who have already encountered it back into its delighting and troubling complexities. Timothy Findley is a major writer at the height of his powers who is consolidating an international reputation for his achievement. A consummate stylist and entertainer, he seems driven to return to a set of private obsessions that electrically connect with the most decisive events of the twentieth century. In choosing to focus on these obsessions and their unfolding in Findley's novels, I provide brief analyses of his published plays, memoir, and short stories but do not discuss them with the thoroughness they deserve. My focus falls on the novels. They provide the most accessible way into Findley's fictional world and represent the work for which he has won most acclaim.

The narrator of Findley's story "Stones" supposes that everyone's life "has its demarcation lines," some marking purely private memories and others that are publicly shared.[1] Findley's fictions explore how these lines are drawn and erased and redrawn through the interplay of individual and communal rememberings. Memory, like art, invokes absence. The photograph is his preferred symbol for the preservation of what is gone, the retrieval of what has been lost, and the survival of memory into an eternal present, but it is a survival marked by ambiguity. In Findley's fiction photographs can never replace words. Instead, they generate more words, as narrators try to understand what lies behind and within the stories that photographs both suggest and hide.

In this book I suggest that the most powerful public demarcation lines of memory in Findley's work are images of the holocaust, which for him encompasses the Nazi concentration camps designed to exterminate whole groups of human beings and the dropping of the atomic bombs on the cities of Japan. These horrific events recall and resituate the repressed histories of violence on which the new world of the Americas was built by European immigrants often fleeing violence yet trailing it in their wake. These historical images expand outward for Findley into other public signs of the misuse of power, such as environmental destruction, and inward into the destructive effects of power and powerlessness on the minds, souls, and bodies of human beings and other living creatures.

Findley's extended examination of the abuses of power involves investigating the psychology of complicity and understanding the misguided human drive for perfection, which in his view reached its ultimate form of expression in fascism. Findley's art is bewildered and fascinated by the many ways in which the monstrous may also be miraculous, and seeks to understand how the dangerousness of beauty, love, and violence may link what propriety teaches should be kept separate.

Paul de Man writes that "modernity exists in the form of a desire to wipe out whatever came earlier, in the hope of reaching at last a point that could be called a true present, a point of origin that marks a new departure."[2] I believe that Findley writes out of his own conflicted love affair with modernity as de Man defines it. His work longs for that "true present" even as it warns against the annihilations that goal may justify. Findley's work constitutes a sustained but loving and sometimes complicitous critique of modernity. Each of his texts may be read as investigating the costs of trying to make such a fresh start, with the earlier texts expressing more sympathy for the annihilating gesture that inaugurates a new Eden and the later texts, beginning with *Not Wanted on the Voyage,* severely castigating the megalomaniacal figures who indulge that desire.

Findley's investigations of the Conradian "secret sharings" of psychiatrist and patient become his most powerful symbols of the spirals of power and desire that lock seeming opposites together in an unfolding drama of surveillance and resistance. The language of mental illness provides his terms of reference. If megalomania becomes his image for imperialist, fascist, and curative models of control, then schizophrenia and autism provide his imagery for the imaginative powers of the weak in eluding ever more ingenious efforts at manipulation and dominance. The asylum becomes his ambiguous image for a dream of safety and renewal gone wrong, just as the Americas represent a similar dream betrayed: the hoped-for paradise of a new world become a killing ground.

With *Headhunter*'s Kurtz, Findley reaches the dead end of the modernist project, taking the horror that Conrad detected in the beginnings of modernism to its logical conclusion in the full flowering of imperialism reached by the death dealing "speculations" of the twentieth century.[3] *The Piano Man's Daughter,* in seeking an earlier beginning in the Edwardian end of empire, comes up against the same dead end of impotence in the legacy of the two world wars. In retreating to the affirmation of the simplest form of survival in the image of human continuity through biological birth, with all its imperfections and uncertainties,

Findley holds the body itself and the mortality it symbolizes as the talisman necessary for reminding human beings to temper their ambitions with mercy, compassion, and tolerance, because they do not exist alone. Individuals are part of a community and rely on communal support for survival.

Animals in Findley's fiction often exist as analogues for the physicality of the human body and as reminders of the interdependence of all species, but they also provide an alternative perspective on life itself. Humor, which in Findley's work is often black or camp, provides another space for locating an agency of resistance. Humor can transform rage into laughter and shift perspectives to reveal the familiar in a new light. Its instabilities further frustrate efforts at control.

Findley takes his stand on the ground of embodied life in the full knowledge that even this ground may be altered by contemporary genetic engineering, plastic and other surgeries, and mind-altering drugs. His texts warn against the dangers of moving too far and too quickly from the legacies bequeathed humanity by cultural traditions that venerate human indebtedness to the natural world. These are humane and conservative ideals that speak directly out of Canadian cultural traditions but that address global concerns of great urgency. Findley's work enacts a complex conversation between the different strands of his inheritance as a twentieth-century writer viewing the world from the relative backwater of Canada. His memoir *Inside Memory* shows how deeply embedded Findley is in a particular Canadian literary culture but also how influenced he has been by American and English mentors. Writing out of his own particular time and place, he seeks a global range of address through a dazzling array of settings, characters, and images.

Acknowledgments

I owe gratitude to my colleagues in Findley studies for their encouragement and example: to John Hulcoop, Eva Marie Kröller, and Laurie Ricou at the University of British Columbia, where I first discovered Findley's fiction and learned to love it; to Anne Bailey and Tom Hastings, whose theses drew me into fresh ways of reading his work; and to Barbara Gabriel and Lorraine York for their steady commitment to expanding the field. My deepest debt is to the group of women who read first drafts of early material, tore it apart, and suggested how to pull it together more sensibly: Christine Bold, Susan Brown, Ann Wilson, and especially Donna Palmateer Pennee, whose wise advice kept me on track during difficult moments. They bear no responsibility for the imprecisions of the final product, however. My debt to my family is deeper than I can acknowledge here. Their love of Findley's fiction and my husband's interest in the theoretical problems he poses for understanding political agency, history, and gender, have been sustaining. Special thanks to Jessica Braden for help with permissions and the index.

I have drawn on my own earlier published work on Findley, as listed in the selected bibliography, repeating sections of some of the arguments but substantially revising the whole.

Quotations from *The Last of the Crazy People, The Butterfly Plague, The Wars, Famous Last Words, Not Wanted on the Voyage, The Telling of Lies, Headhunter, The Piano Man's Daughter, You Went Away, Inside Memory: Pages from a Writer's Workbook, Dinner along the Amazon, Dust to Dust,* and *Stones,* by Timothy Findley. © 1967, 1969, 1986, 1977, 1981, 1984, 1986, 1993, 1995, 1996, 1990, 1984, 1988, 1997 by Pebble Productions, Inc. Published by HarperCollins Publishers, Ltd. Quotations from *Can You See Me Yet?* by Timothy Findley. © 1977 by Pebble Productions, Inc. Published by Talonbooks. Quotations from *The Stillborn Lover* and *The Trials of Ezra Pound,* by Timothy Findley. © 1993, 1994 by Pebble Productions, Inc. Published by Blizzard. All rights reserved. Used by permission.

Chronology

1978–1979   Writer in residence at the University of Toronto.

1979   *Sir John A.—Himself!* produced in London, Ontario. *Dieppe, 1942,* by Findley and Whitehead, broadcast on CBC Radio; wins ANIK Best Documentary Award.

1981   *Famous Last Words* published.

1982   Receives an honorary degree from Trent University. His father dies.

1983   *The Wars* is filmed.

1984   *Dinner along the Amazon* published. Receives an honorary degree from the University of Guelph.

1985   *Not Wanted on the Voyage* published. Receives Canadian Authors Association Award.

1986   Revised edition of *The Butterfly Plague* and *The Telling of Lies* published. Made an Officer of the Order of Canada. Elected Canadian President of PEN International. Wins CNIB Talking Book of the Year Award for *Not Wanted on the Voyage.*

1988   *Stones* published. Receives Ontario Trillium Award. Radio adaptation of *Famous Last Words* broadcast.

1989   Wins Trillium Award for *Stones,* Edgar Award for *The Telling of Lies,* and National Radio Award for adaptation of *Famous Last Words.*

1990   *Inside Memory: Pages from a Writer's Workbook* published. His mother dies.

1991   Receives Canadian Authors Association Literary Award for *Inside Memory.* Named to the Order of Ontario.

1992   *Not Wanted on the Voyage* made into a play. The National Film Board produces a film about his life and writing.

1993   *Headhunter* published. *The Stillborn Lover* produced and published.

1994   Receives City of Toronto Book Award for *Headhunter* and Chalmers Award for *The Stillborn Lover.*

1995   *The Piano Man's Daughter* published.

1996   *You Went Away* published. Made a Knight of the Order of Arts and Letters by the French government. Begins dividing his time between Ontario and France.

1997   *Dust to Dust* published.

Chapter One
Surviving the Holocaust

Findley's Fictional World

What are the elements that have made Timothy Findley one of Canada's most popular and esteemed writers? Many critics remark upon details of craft: the power of visual imagery, the filmic attention to gesture, the playwright's ear for dialogue, and the storyteller's love of narrative. These stylistic strengths are mobilized in the service of what strikes many readers as a powerfully compelling vision, a vision at once compulsive and ambivalent in its repetitions of the marks of the Findley signature: desire, madness, war, fire, fascism, the holocaust, and nuclear annihilation. Findley confesses: "I want edge."[1] That desire for edge and the edge that his works achieve determine the responses of his admirers and detractors alike. Findley's edge involves lodging "an anchor in the *real* heart, the *real* spirit and the *real* turmoil of *real* life" (Kruk, 125). With that anchor secured, Findley then feels free to develop a theatrical style that floats away from reality to create larger-than-life people and gestures that give "both comic edge and tragic dimensions" to his writing (Kruk, 126). Findley seems to care most about the emotional impact of his work, and his writing seems driven by an urgent belief that his stories can influence how his readers perceive their own roles in the world.

In interviews and speeches, Findley is an articulate expositor of his own work. He expresses a desire for ecological, social, and political peace, advocating respect for groups who have been socially ignored or undervalued: children, animals, women, those defined as differently abled or mentally ill, and those defined as racial others by a dominant white hegemony. He is suspicious of power and those who exercise it, and particularly contemptuous of the models for successful masculinity that win approbation in North American culture. Because his own explications of his work are so articulate and persuasive, many critics are tempted to rely on Findley's own explanations for describing his work. Although it is interesting to compare Findley's accounts of his intentions in writing a story or play to one's own reactions and to other critical accounts of that same work, Findley's readings cannot be taken as definitive. They must be tested against the usual standards of evidence in judging literary value and achievement. Like all readings of a literary work, Findley's own interpretations of his work are only partial in their ability to describe his achievement. Additionally, writers are seldom the best critical readers of what they have achieved because of their invest- ment in the process and product. Findley has said, for example, that he wants his writing to argue for peace, yet his books are so powerful pre- cisely because they express an ambivalence about violence, creating con- tradictory emotions of fascination and horror through scenes of violence, excess, and abjection. Although he despises the crassness of those who openly seek and worship money, his stories reveal a fascination with the lives of the rich and the luxury that money can buy. He is a storyteller, after all, and the apparently clear statements of his interviews become muddied in the context of the human dilemmas developed in his fiction. Ultimately, it is his skill in staging conflict and reproducing ambivalence that draws readers to his works again and again. Findley's comments, then, are best read as further extensions of the fiction rather than as explanatory glosses on it. To take this approach is not to question Find- ley's good faith in any way but rather to recognize the complexity of the issues his work addresses.

This book has been conceived as a kind of travel guide for the reader who plans to visit or revisit the imaginary world created by Findley's fic- tion. In recognition of the imaginative geography that an accomplished writer can create through narrative, Findley titles one of the stories in *Dinner along the Amazon* "Hello Cheeverland, Goodbye." This story is prefaced by a quotation from the writer Findley has invented as an alter ego for himself, Nicholas Fagan. Fagan suggests that people are actually taking up residence in "Cheeverland," the imaginative territory obses- sively delineated in Cheever's stories, because it is so compellingly real. In his preface to the collection, Findley elaborates on this concept, argu- ing that "the pursuit of an obsession through the act of writing is not so much a question of repetition as it is of regeneration."[2] To read his own writing, he implies, is like entering into Findleyland. We recognize the landscape and the familiar features, but because the writer never tires of these obsessions neither does his reader. These familiar elements are always "freshly seething with possibilities" (x). Findley's nine novels, one novella, three collections of short stories, and several plays compose the geography of a landscape that derives its edge from the ways in which it both creates its own world and comments upon our own.

This book argues that the defining obsession of Findley's fictional universe is the experience of the holocaust, which for Findley means the Nazi concentration camps and the Allied dropping of the nuclear bombs on Japan. In different ways, each of his books asks the same questions: How did this happen? How can we prevent such things from happening again? How does one continue living in a world where such things can happen? How can a writer articulate the unspeakable? How can humanity survive the holocaust?

Findleyland is a world of recognizable landmarks, each of which is scarred by history. The title of Findley's book-length memoir, *Inside Memory: Pages from a Writer's Workbook,* asserts the importance of the act of remembrance through reconceiving memory as a place one must enter. The writer enters memory so that the reader may enter story. To be outside memory is to be lost, shut out from continuity with one's history and one's place. To forget, then, is also to be forgotten. The writer's task is to join us together in memory, enabling a communal survival and a communal remembering, because to forget is also to neglect the responsibilities of witnessing. To witness, in Findley's vision, is part of both his thematics and his strategy.

But to be "inside memory" can also suggest a sanctuary from the horrors of the outside world, or, less positively, a retreat from the world of the present into a private space dedicated to the past. In what ways are these two ideas compatible? How can the same book be both a retreat and a witnessing? How can a character perform his or her witnessing, which is usually perceived as an intervention into public space, through a private retreat into madness, which is normally seen as the space furthest removed from the world of the real? In Findley's fiction, these boundaries are repeatedly transgressed and thrown into question. Madness is often privileged as the highest form of truth telling and the space occupied by the visionary. Far from being on the fringes of the world, the mad or those deemed mad by those with the power to enforce that naming are at its true center, and they pay the cost for that centrality.

These are some of the issues that Findley asks his readers to contemplate and this is the vision of his work that he invites his readers to share. His novels are inscribed by conflicting messages, and to some extent, how we unpack their meanings depends on the values we bring to the texts. As literary theorists bring forth new modes of reading, academic criticism of Findley's work is uncovering further layers of complexity in his fictions and reconsidering the kind of cultural work that his texts perform in our society. My critical language here signals the shift in contemporary theory away from authorial intention toward reader response. Literary texts typically perform different kinds of cultural work in a community. They may substantiate some dominant assumptions while challenging others. Findley's novels create a community of readers who share the experience of immersion in his fictional world, the world of Findleyland. Critics disagree in describing how Findleyland shapes its communities of readers. The experience of reading Findley's texts is being described in different ways by feminist, postcolonial, psychoanalytic, and queer theorists. Each theory brings its own questions to the texts and finds its own answers in them. This book will explain and assess how some of these new approaches interpret Findley's fiction. It would be interesting to learn more about those outside of academia who read Findley's work and why they find it entertaining and important, but such a study is beyond the scope of this book, which will focus on the critical reception of Findley's texts and the changing ways that academic critics are interpreting them.

Findley's work has drawn the dedicated attention of a number of superb critics, many of them women particularly interested in his depiction of female characters. Findley's fictions often include strongly valorized central female characters whose voices, perspectives, and judgments usually carry authorial endorsement. Some critics think that Findley's women are idealized. In the dynamics of good and evil that his fictions often invoke, women are usually cast on the side of the good. Some critics, such as Lorna Irvine and Lorraine York, have concluded that Findley's work can be described as feminist because his writing shares, with feminism, a strong distrust of patriarchal values and the social order they support. Other critics, such as Barbara Gabriel, Tom Hastings, and Donna Pennee, argue that Findley's critique of patriarchy is less interested in arguing for the equality of women than it is in critiquing the social definitions of masculinity available to men in patriarchal cultures such as Europe and North America. Such readers are more skeptical about the ambivalent portrayals of gender roles and of human sexuality in Findley's fiction. His characterizations of women often confirm misogynist stereotypes linking good women to the natural world and to nurturing and life-affirming values in opposition to male violence. Findley's nonendorsed bad women, on the other hand, are usually women like *Headhunter*'s Freda Manley, who has learned to succeed in the world of men on male terms. His plots often employ childbirth as a shorthand metaphor for affirming the continuity of humane values in the face of a civilization increasingly committed to death under the rule of men. A reliance on plotting that casts good women chiefly as ineffective agents (although morally strong), or as primarily important for their ability to reproduce the race through childbirth, risks reinforcing stereotypes of women as being without agency except that which is biologically determined. More work needs to be done on representations of gender in Findley's fiction and plays, and on readers' reception of these texts, before Findley's contribution to rethinking gender roles can be more fully elaborated.

Nonetheless, it seems clear that Findley's novels create a concerted demythologization of the white, middle-class, heterosexual, nuclear family that has enjoyed a privileged place in North American ideology. Simon During argues that "the heterosexual family was the social unit most easily transplanted into and across colonial settlements; it ensured the reproduction of the vulnerable white society. It ordered women's lives in particular."[3] For During, this colonial history explains why the family shapes Nobel Prize-winning author Patrick White's "identification with the national culture" (27), which for White was Australia, despite White's own nontraditional choice of a dedicated homosexual relationship. I believe that the same holds true for Findley. Canadian national culture, and the larger Western culture of which it forms a part, are explained in his fictions through a version of the Freudian family romance in which fathers are blamed for both abusing and abdicating their paternal power, mothers are usually punished but not overtly blamed, and children are usually forgiven for the different ways they seek to escape the pain that these variously negligent fathers and mothers inflict.

The first two books that look critically at Findley's writing have constructed different, but complementary, routes into understanding his work. Lorraine York's *Front Lines: The Fiction of Timothy Findley* argues that "[i]f one thinks of modern war as a text which has articulated the horrendous 'possibilities' of our culture, then the fictions of Timothy Findley participate fully and passionately in the 'discursive space' which that grim text has inscribed."[4] Using this expanded notion of war as more than just a historical event, she suggests that all of Findley's work is unified by the notion of war as the defining text of Western male civilization. Novels and plays written by Findley since York's book came out in 1991 confirm these insights but force a modification to the chronological pattern she detected, seeing Findley's novels move from the First World War to the Second World War to the Nuclear Age in "a path which itself narrates the march of modern history towards an ever increasingly mechanized and brutal form of war" (xxii). With Findley's most recent writing, the chronological line identified by York loops back upon itself, returning to the period of the First World War in *The Piano Man's Daughter* (1995) and to the Second World War, the time of Findley's own childhood, in *You Went Away* (1996). Yet Findley's vocabulary of war is less the historian's than it is a Yeatsian late romantic's vocabulary of prophecy and plague, of cataclysmic endings and apocalypse.

Donna Palmateer Pennee's *Moral Metafiction: Counterdiscourse in the Novels of Timothy Findley* examines Findley's "use of metafictive devices to write about specifically moral issues and morally problematic periods in history."[5] She coins the term "moral metafiction" to describe (and resolve) an apparent contradiction in Findley's work: On the one hand, it is metafictionally self-conscious (aware that it is "fiction 'about' fictions, about the construction of discourses" [19]); on the other hand, it is morally driven to counter some dominant systems of discourse that structure our understanding of the world, suggesting that some choices, however constructed, are preferable to others. In other words, she sees the texts' stance as desiring closure, the choice of one option over another as morally superior, even as they display a simultaneous awareness that to seek such closure is to make an arbitrary and possibly repressive decision. Following Linda Hutcheon's description of how postmodernism functions, Pennee solves this problem of the contradiction in Findley's work by arguing that Findley's texts pose the dilemma of moral decision making as one that readers must make for themselves, but she is clearly not satisfied with this way out of the dilemma. Nonetheless, this ambitious study openly addresses the central question all Findley criticism seeks to negotiate either directly or indirectly: What is the "political effect" of Findley's texts (12)? Pennee's study opens this discussion for further investigation in a meticulously theorized and exciting way.

The idea of intertextuality, an important element in York's and Pennee's discussions of Findley's work, is highlighted in Anne Geddes Bailey's manuscript *Dangerous Acts: Intertextual Ambivalence in the Novels of Timothy Findley* (still unpublished at the time of writing but expected to appear in 1998). She reads "psychiatry, religion, economics, politics, law, and fascism as texts in intertextual dialogue with Findley's texts" to point out the centrality of reading as a political act in Findley's address to the reader, and to call attention to the ways in which his novels insist on their relation to a social, historical, and political world outside the literary text.[6] In other words, what Findley terms his "anchors" in the real world can be seen as social text in dialogue with the literary texts he creates.

Most work on Findley addresses the social, historical, and political elements of his work, but only recently has criticism turned toward analysis of the politics of gender and how they are played out in his fiction. Feminist and queer theorists are generating new readings of his work and forcing a reconsideration of how his books interrogate and participate in both dominant heterosexual discourses and in resistant discourses of gender relations. Part of this activity involves rethinking the roles of family, violence, and expressive gesture in Findley's fiction. Tom Hastings, in a Ph.D. thesis titled "Into the Fire: Masculinities and Militarism in Timothy Findley's 'The Wars,' " argues that "the misuse of authority by patriarchal figures, especially the suffering that they cause their 'sons,' is . . . *the* central thematic in all of Findley's work."[7] Anne Geddes Bailey is now studying the neglected roles of mothers in Findley's fiction. Citing Eve Sedgwick's groundbreaking work on gender, Barbara Gabriel argues that Findley's work is characterized by a "double weaving in which a submerged . . . gay text both informs and operates in tension with the dominant narrative."[8] Reading for the "double weave" helps bring Findley's early texts, which often puzzled critics, into sharper focus, and it changes how we conceptualize the patterns of his work as a whole.

But the attentiveness to gender and its construction through discourse is part of a larger concern with power in general reflected in Findley's works. Findley's homosexuality is only one element in the repertoire of lived experience he brings to his writing. This study suggests that nation and class are equally important elements in the heady mix Findley offers his readers. Findley's treatment of race has attracted very little commentary, yet race as a concept and racially marked figures haunt the margins, and occasionally take center stage, in all of his texts.

Public and Private Contexts

It is probably impossible for either Findley or the academic critic to understand fully the personal investments that charge his writing, but it is important to try to unpack these as best we can with the evidence we have. Wrestling with the particular details of his life, Findley records his own intensely personal readings of the significance of his time and place in much of his writing.

He was born on 30 October 1930 in a spacious house in a well-to-do inner-city neighborhood of Toronto, Rosedale, which, with its gracious houses, social pretensions, and treed ravines, provides the setting for most of Findley's fiction. His grandfather, Thomas Findley, had been an important figure in the small city of Toronto, serving as president of Massey-Harris from 1917 to the time of his death in 1921. (Massey-Harris was "at that time the largest farm-machinery manufacturer in the British Empire,"[9] but more than this, the Massey family has since become one of the chief signifiers for the interrelations of class privilege, wealth, and patronage of the arts in Canada. They created two performance halls in Toronto, Massey Hall and Hart House. Vincent Massey, chairman of the Royal Commission on National Development in the Arts, Letters and Sciences, also called the Massey Commission, issued the commission's groundbreaking report in 1951, identifying American mass entertainment as a major threat to Canadian culture and recommending such countermeasures as the establishment of the National Library and the Canada Council. Much of the flowering of culture and higher education in Canada has resulted from the institution of the various recommendations made in this report [Roberts, 11].) After Thomas Findley died, the Findleys experienced economic difficulties. Findley's father, Allan, the younger son, was a stockbroker who was forced to reduce expenses after the stock market crash of 1929, including moving his family to a smaller, rented home.

Findley has drawn heavily on his own family history in much of his writing. His Uncle Tiff, his father's older brother for whom Timothy Findley was named, had returned an invalid from the First World War. Uncle Tiff's life and the letters he sent home were the inspiration for Findley's most famous novel, *The Wars,* and it is from him that Findley received not only his proper name but also the nickname Tiff, a name his friends still use for him. *The Piano Man's Daughter* is based in part on Findley's mother's family, the Bulls. Margaret Bull's father owned a piano factory, and Margaret met Findley's father on a piano bench.

Findley has often spoken of the searing sense of abandonment and helplessness he felt when his father enlisted for the Second World War without telling him first. That emotional trauma is detailed most openly in *You Went Away*, but it may be traced in almost everything Findley has written. Although very discreet, Carol Roberts's biography of Findley has made new details of his life available for critical use. But tracing connections between the life and the work is of limited interest unless it also illuminates the creative process through which life is made into art. Findley's own memoir, *Inside Memory,* provides his perspective on that process but it is necessarily a partial and fragmented view.

Using all these sources, the critic can see how the specificities of Findley's time and place not only survive within his work but also form its determinant patterns. Public and domestic events are equally important influences. Findley's concerns are with the most widely debated issues of contemporary times, but they are mediated through a personal, and sometimes almost a cryptically private, mythology. Findley's fiction addresses serious social problems: the surviving legacy of fascism, the nature of progress, the degree of individual responsibility to be assumed for collective decisions, the balancing of public and private good, the hypocrisy and truth in celebrating family values. At times, he moves these social issues into the realm of the sacred, recasting them as questions about the existence and provenance of evil and the meaning of life and death. He approaches these issues in full awareness of their complexity, but in an instinctive sense of alliance with the underdog.

Paradoxically, his central characters are almost always marginalized figures: children, mad people, watchers, women, a cat. The narrative stance is usually that of the witness, someone who watches but is powerless to intervene or unable to distinguish clearly the meaning of an action observed. Findley's writing both captures that childhood sense of powerlessness in the face of an inscrutable adult world and tries to counter it by assuming the power of the pen. His writing affirms the belief that to tell a story is to intervene in determining the survival of a point of view that might otherwise disappear. But it also resonates with awareness of how fraught any act of interpretation must be.

In the story "Dust," the central character Oliver waves to a stranger on a boat and is initially elated that this is the first time he has waved to anyone since his companion René has died. But later, overhearing a woman's despairing appeal to her husband, he wonders if his wave was a gesture meaning "[n]ot *hello*—but *goodbye*. To everything."[10] In his current state of grief, even he cannot be sure. Findley recurrently employs the act of waving as a sign for the difficulty of interpreting gesture when the watcher has no access to the intention of the person waving, but more importantly, the acts of recognition and farewell are intimately connected in this ambiguous gesture. Findley's fiction often evokes nostalgia for a past, or perhaps an illusion of innocence associated with the past, that now seems irrevocably lost. He wants readers to perform the double gesture of the wave: simultaneously to recognize what has been lost in moving forward from the past while learning to leave it behind or save it in memory.

The threat of apocalypse, the inevitable ending of a culture's way of life or of the world itself, shapes everything that Timothy Findley has written. A mood combining nostalgia and apocalypse can be seen to characterize colonial discourse as well as the temper of the postholocaust era to which Findley consciously ascribes both characteristics, though he remains acutely aware of Canada's colonial heritage and how it has affected Canadian culture. Canada was formed by the confederation of several British colonies and the conquered territory of Quebec, which had been a French colony, on land originally bartered from First Nations peoples through a series of treaties that were never properly honored by their European signators. Although Canada dates its birth as a nation from 1867, it attained full independence through a long process of gradual changes that culminated in the "repatriating" of the constitution (when a Canadian Constitution was substituted for the British North America Act, which until then had governed the nation from Britain) in 1982. Unlike the United States, Canada never experienced a revolution to create a sharp break with British institutional structures and traditions. As a result, a colonial mentality survived among English Canadians long into the twentieth century. Indeed, Canadian citizenship was not established until after the Second World War, in 1947.

Some believe that the crucible of war, and especially the massive deaths on the battlefields of Belgium during the First World War, commemorated in John McCrae's famous poem "In Flanders Fields" (1919), helped Canada move psychologically from colony to nation. Support for their view comes from the fact that Canada became a separate signatory to the League of Nations in 1919. Others argue that this shift occurred much later, at the time of the Second World War, when Canada claimed the right to declare war on its own rather than automatically finding itself at war through Britain's declaration. Others see the massive Canadian sacrifice of lives at the battle of Dieppe (1942) as the decisive moment defining the birth of the nation. In the short story "Stones," Findley's narrator explains that for Canadians, "This was our Waterloo. Our Gettysburg" (*Stones,* 215). Findley, along with most Canadians, is well aware of the importance of both world wars in creating a sense of Canadian national identity.

Therefore, despite Canada's declared self-image as a "peaceable kingdom," an image popularized by Northrop Frye and given political shape in Canadian prime minister Lester Pearson's formation of the United Nations Peace Force system in 1956, Canadian national identity is intimately tied to the idea of war as the rite of passage through which the colony becomes a nation. Such a formula, of course, assumes that human identity is masculine identity, and that full masculine identity is achieved through violence. Yet if the nation finds itself as a fully matured entity through war, as conventional wisdom would have it, the events of the Second World War have shown that the price for such national bonding is the loss of a larger notion of humanity.

Findley believes that with the dropping of the atomic bombs on Hiroshima and Nagasaki, in 1945, "our moral concept of horror was altered forever."[11] He begins *Inside Memory* with a chapter on the significance of Remembrance Day. In a later chapter, he writes, "Mine was the generation whose childhood had been interrupted by the war. . . . Our childhood ended with the dropping of the Hiroshima bomb."[12] He concludes *Inside Memory*, out of chronological sequence, with the story of a time shortly after the war when, visiting a house in Hollywood, he stumbled upon photographs taken by the first official army photographer through the gates of Dachau after its liberation. He writes: "Even in a world where Nagasaki and Hiroshima, Dachau and Auschwitz are names that tell of horrors distant as the Inquisition, it cannot be told what it meant to see those photographs that night" (*Memory*, 310). Findley's work can be read as a lifetime of trying to articulate what cannot be told: what he terms here the "appalling intimacy" of being forced "into the company of murderers" (*Memory*, 310–11). Believing that it is dangerous "to become inured to the way of the world" (*Memory*, 313), he seeks through his writing to recreate in his readers that first sense of shock, outrage, and horrified complicity that he felt in viewing those photographs of atrocity. For him it seems to be the experiential equivalent of Robert Ross's rape in *The Wars*, or Ruth's discovery of her brother's pornography lodged within the pages of his favorite children's stories in *The Butterfly Plague:* to be assaulted where you feel most safe. For Findley, the impact of this experience is heightened by the fact that he first saw the Dachau photographs in Hollywood, a place symbolic of glamour and success, everything that seems antithetical to the horrors of the Nazi death camps, and that he saw these images of human hatred and violence while listening to light music celebrating human love. Much of his writing seeks to recreate that heightened sense of contradiction at the heart of experience, how terrible opposites so often dwell together. The argument of this book is that all of Findley's writing is profoundly marked by the revelations of the holocaust and the dropping of the atomic bombs. Everything he has written addresses two questions: After such knowledge, how can we go on? How can we survive the holocaust?

These dramatic historic events that shaped Findley's childhood and his passage into adulthood have remained touchstones for him through-

out his career. In the early works, they are sometimes evoked in a manner so personal as to seem obscure or forced, but in the later works their
power is effectively realized. These experiences would be enough to
guarantee the centrality of loss, abandonment, and horror in Findley's
fiction and the corresponding need to affirm, celebrate, and protect
endangered species, including the human, from disaster, but there are
other elements of Findley's heritage that contribute to the emotional
resonance of such Findley catchwords, used repeatedly in his fiction, as
"Forever," "Never," and "Against Despair."

If the atomic bomb represents one of those watersheds of history that
alters forever how people understand their world, and for Findley also
marked his own passage into maturity, then the First World War can be
seen as another such moment, both for Western civilization and for
Findley personally. Although he was born long after this war had ended,
he saw its impact everywhere: on his Uncle Tiff, on literary modernism,
and on Canadian nationalism. In the mythology of modernism, the First
World War marked a decisive break with a genteel past and the beginnings of modernity. In the mythology of Canadian nationalism, the First
World War marked Canada's passage from colony to nation, adolescent
to adult. Findley's fiction complicates the nationalist reading by incor-
porating the dissenting English war poets' belief that this war marked
the betrayal and slaughter of a younger generation by its elders. The
war destroyed a world of class privilege and order to install instead a
world where money alone ruled, regardless of its pedigree. Findley's
characters are often wealthy, but he draws a sharp distinction between
old money, which is usually good, and new money, which is often ques-
tionable. This snobbish adherence to outdated touchstones of moral
worth through attitudes to money makes the surface textures of Findley's narratives remarkably rich in telling detail, but at the cost of com-
plicating the value systems his texts advocate.

A suspicion of violent solutions to national quarrels, a questioning of
the costs of progress, and a conservative attachment to tradition mark
the difference between Canada's United Empire Loyalist heritage and
that of the American Revolution in the United States. Many Canadian
writers, particularly in southern Ontario, have felt an affinity for the
mythos of the American South, even as they abhor the system of slavery
on which that myth depended for its very survival. In the mythology of
the American South, the Civil War marked a moment of decisive rup-
ture where progress and nostalgia were clearly at odds. Findley's *The
Last of the Crazy People* dramatizes the ambivalent sense of connection he

feels between the obsolescence of the Winslow family's faded gentility (so similar to that of his own family) and the genteel aura of the Old South, also doomed to extinction. The Winslow family's eroding privilege and dysfunctional dynamics is repeated, with variations, in the situation of the Damarosch family in *The Butterfly Plague,* the Ross family in *The Wars,* the Mauberleys in *Famous Last Words,* the habitués of the Atlantic House Hotel in *The Telling of Lies,* the Kilworths in *The Piano Man's Daughter,* and the Forbeses in *You Went Away.* In each case, parental abandonment and abdication of responsibility lead to nostalgia for what might have been. The helplessness and incomprehension of the child in such situations, most starkly created in the 11-year-old Hooker of *The Last of the Crazy People* and the nine-year-old Matthew in *You Went Away,* can be read as suggesting that "there is something odd about the children of the rich who have been abandoned, one way or another, by their parents" (*Memory,* 119) , but it may also serve as a marker of a colonial self-characterization that still appeals to many Canadians' sense of themselves.

The dominant parental metaphor of settler colonialism names the imperial power a "mother" country and the colony a child. During both world wars, in key disastrous battles, the colonial "children," Australia and Canada, felt abandoned and betrayed by the British officers who ordered their soldiers to their deaths. Findley's work can affect its readers so powerfully in part because it can make private stories of individuals resonate with the emotional sense of abandonment felt by an entire country.

The Life and Work

Critics have paid considerable attention to the influence of Findley's early training and work as a dancer and actor on his fiction, but less attention has been paid to his Canadian and southern Ontario roots, the class background of his family, and his relationship with his lifelong companion, William Whitehead, whom he met in 1962, and who serves as first reader, editor, and critic for everything that Findley writes. A study of their collaboration is overdue. It was after meeting Whitehead that Findley decided to leave the theater for life as a writer, finishing his first novel, *The Last of the Crazy People,* in 1964. The same year they moved to Stone Orchard, a farm in the country northeast of Toronto, where they lived until they felt they could no longer manage such a big property as they grew older, reluctantly putting it up for sale in 1996.

The Spring 1997 advertising insert in the Toronto newspaper *The Globe and Mail* describes the property as follows: "FAMOUS STONE ORCHARD NR. LAKE SIMCOE $479,000. Loved retreat of Timothy Findley. 50 acres of fields, woods, huge pond overlooked by gazebo, 2 barns & historic 5 bedroom rambling house + inground pool, 3 car carport." Clearly the name of Timothy Findley and the aura of his lifestyle carry the cachet of a star in Canada. His name sells not only books and theatrical shows but even real estate. Another part of the reason for selling the property was apparently a need for more privacy to write uninterrupted by visits and requests from an admiring public. Findley and Whitehead now live part of the year in France.

But Findley was not always so popular. After failing to find a publisher for *The Last of the Crazy People* in Canada, Findley published the novel in the United States in 1967 where, according to Carol Roberts, "[I]t sold moderately well and won critical praise" (Roberts, 53). The Canadian reception was less positive. *The Butterfly Plague* followed a similar pattern of American acceptance and Canadian rejection when it appeared in 1969. It received only two reviews in Canada, one positive and one negative, both by the writer Marian Engel, who was later to become a close personal friend of Findley. The story illustrates how small and potentially incestuous the literary world of Canada was at the time, and how unprepared it was to understand Findley's distinctive and challenging vision.

Many of Findley's novels produce a profound sense of category confusion, unbalancing reader's attempts to "place" the text within a known order. When *The Butterfly Plague* first appeared, Canadian critics wondered why a Canadian was writing about Hollywood. National boundaries had been breached. Similarly, many of Findley's novels challenged attempts to pigeonhole them into traditional literary genre categories while generating many questions about his recurring themes and devices. Is *The Last of the Crazy People* a murder story or a love story? Is *The Telling of Lies* really a murder mystery? Does *The Wars* confirm or challenge the genre of the war story? What is the function of the anachronisms in *Not Wanted on the Voyage*? How can literary characters from other novels come to life within the apparent realism of *Headhunter*? Why is cross-dressing so recurrent an element throughout Findley's fictions? Why do so many of his characters carry names that seem to betray rather than reveal their assigned gender? Why are filmic, stage, and advertising techniques such a prominent cross-generic element in Findley's work? What functions do all these different kinds of category crossings perform? These are the kinds of questions Findley's work provokes in his readers, questions I explore in the following chapters.

Findley himself has worked as an actor and a writer, crossing over from the stage to the study in the course of his career. His first job as an actor was with Kingston's International Players during their first winter season in Toronto (1951–1952). In 1953 he played some minor roles in two Shakespeare plays in the inaugural season of the Stratford Shakespeare Festival in Canada. His work so impressed Alec Guinness that he provided Findley with financial assistance to attend classes at London's Central School of Speech and Drama. After he graduated in 1954, Findley worked on contract playing several roles in the United Kingdom for the next two years. During this time he worked on his first publication as a writer, the short story "About Effie" (about one of the maids who worked in his house when he was a child). This appeared in the first issue of the *Tamarack Review* (Autumn 1956), a literary journal that became an important promoter of Canadian literature. The start of Findley's career coincided, then, with a renewed sense of national identity and interest in the literature of his country.

Findley also found encouragement among prominent American actors, writers, and literary agents. Thornton Wilder was a particularly powerful and enduring influence. Findley went to Hollywood in 1956, where he found some work acting and doctoring scripts and where he continued to write. He returned to Toronto in 1958. Findley was writing advertising copy at the radio station CFGM in Richmond Hill, Toronto, and arts news for CBC Radio's *The Learning Stage* during the time he wrote his first two novels. In 1967 Findley wrote the script for *The Paper People,* the Canadian Broadcasting Corporation's first feature-length color film for television, coproduced with the National Film Board of Canada. According to critic Mary Jane Miller, the critical response was violently mixed, with critics either loving it or hating it. Reviewing the script and the film in the 1980s, Miller concluded that it had been underrated and neglected, finding it "one of the best television dramas broadcast in the thirty years of CBC television drama."[13] This film about the making of a documentary film exploring the work of an artist who makes disposable art, papier mâché people who are created to be burned, questions the claims to authenticity of both documentary and the creative arts. In 1974 Findley became the first playwright in residence at the National Arts Centre in Ottawa, writing and staging the play *Can You See Me Yet?* in 1975. Both of these scripts address themes of personal, artistic, and national identity through imagery of madness and the destructive and cleansing powers of fire, elements that continue to operate as touchstones of Findley's imaginative vision.

During this period, Findley was also painting for his own satisfaction. His paintings, like his writing, are motivated by an interest in exploring what he calls "attitude," which lies in gesture or the way people present themselves."[14] He paints what is in his mind, not "something out the window" (Alice, 11). These comments illuminate his narrative strategy in *The Wars,* where Robert's character is defined through a series of photographic images that have captured gestures in which the researcher hopes to read the essence of a life. The first Findley novel to be published in Canada, *The Wars* appeared in 1977 and won the Governor General's Award, Canada's most prestigious literary prize at that time. It was made into a feature film for which Findley wrote the screenplay in 1981. Throughout this period (1971–1980) Findley was also writing television scripts, sometimes with his partner William Whitehead. His script for *Whiteoaks of Jalna* adapted the work of Canadian writer Mazo de la Roche. The Alliance of Canadian Cinema, Television, and Radio Artists (ACTRA)-award-winning series *The National Dream* dramatized Canadian history, as did *The Newcomers* and *Dieppe 1942*. The TV drama *Other People's Children*, written in 1978, examined the relationships of a psychiatrist who works with autistic children, a theme that recurs in the novel *Headhunter* and in the short story "Dreams."

From 1977 to 1978 Findley served as chairman of the Writers Union of Canada, Canada's leading organization of writers. His play *John A.— Himself* was performed at Theatre London in 1979. Sir John A. Macdonald was Canada's first prime minister. Findley adopted a vaudeville approach to convey Macdonald looking back on his life and seeing it as theatrical performance. Reviews were mixed and the play has not been published. With positive reviews and publication abroad, *Famous Last Words* firmly established Findley's international reputation when it appeared in 1981. Findley adapted the novel to be broadcast in five one-hour segments by CBC Radio in 1988. *Dinner along the Amazon,* his first collection of short stories, and *Not Wanted on the Voyage,* his fictional rewriting of the story of Noah's flood, both appeared in 1984. *Voyage* was adapted for the stage as a play of the same name in 1987. From 1986 to 1987 Findley served as the president of the English Canadian center of PEN International, a writer's organization that promotes human rights through publicizing and advocating for the release of writers who have been unjustly imprisoned for their work throughout the world.

In 1986 Findley published the revised version of *The Butterfly Plague*. In his introduction to this rewriting of his earlier novel, Findley suggests that the first version suffered from the writer's form of stage fright: page-fright. "It was a good idea, but its time had not come. Or rather, its writer had not made sure of his craft. He simply wrote it too soon."[15] The writer sure of his craft is evident in the stylistic virtuosity of the stories in *Stones*, published in 1988, and in the experiment with the mystery genre in *The Telling of Lies*, published in 1989. *Inside Memory*, a midlife memoir, appeared in 1990. *Headhunter*, in 1993, shocked many readers with the savagery of its subject matter and the bleakness of its vision. Two plays, *The Stillborn Lover* (1993), produced for the stage, and *The Trials of Ezra Pound* (1994), written for radio (and aired on CBC Stereo in 1990), introduce further Findleyesque variations on betrayals both personal and public. These plays use the past to make pointed commentary on the problems of the present. But the darkening vision that seemed to intensify with each book after the publication of *Stones* suddenly lightens again with *The Piano Man's Daughter* (1995), a family chronicle with a relatively happy ending. *You Went Away* (1996), although a sadder book, repeats the mood of nostalgic return to earlier times. The collected stories of *Dust to Dust* (1997), however, return to that obsession with mortality that in retrospect can be seen as haunting everything Findley has written.

Timothy Findley is a writer in midcareer and at the height of his powers. It is impossible to predict what he will publish next. In what follows, I trace the contours of the fictional worlds he creates for his readers and the emotional chords these worlds strike. Findley is often termed a postmodernist writer, yet despite his use of many techniques currently associated with postmodernism his work also challenges several of the key tenets of a postmodernist aesthetic. Findley shares the postmodern belief that social roles, including gender roles, are constructed rather than biologically determined, but the novels and plays through which he develops his understanding of the complex ways in which such roles are constructed appeal to notions of truth and reality that postmodernism would deny. Findley's novels, stories, and plays share what postmodernists would call an old-fashioned attention to the centrality of character. Although the instability of language as a signifying system remains an important element in his work, his fiction and drama begin and end with people who seem to take on lives of their own beyond the words that have created them on the page.

Findley tells Donald Cameron "All authors are whispered to by their characters. The characters want life, and you have to give it to them. It's a little like rape, with no recourse to abortion. They take your body, and you have to give birth."[16] This romantic image of literary creation as an act of violent bodily possession moves the author beyond conventional gender assignments and privileges the act of creation over the creator, who becomes a mediator and facilitator rather than an initiator of the work of art. Findley explores this notion of the artist as medium most fully in his characterization of Lilah Kemp in *Headhunter.* For Findley, to be a writer is a heroic and dangerous calling. He writes "I know that the human imagination can save us; save the human race and save all the rest that is alive and save this place—the earth—that is itself alive" (*Memory,* 314). This sounds like a messianic task. Findley's fiction explores the allure and dangers of conjuring such power, fully aware of the ways in which the author is both like a god and a megalomaniac. In urging readers to save the earth, his texts most often show the evil and unintended effects of such idealism. His dedication to the celebration of life and the infinite possibilities of the imagination leads him, therefore, to create a variety of experimental texts, each of which draws the reader away from certainty toward complexity, and away from a focus on the writer toward the work.

Chapter Two
Innocence and Complicity

After the horror of the holocaust, a civilization's engineered attempt to destroy an entire race of people, many writers wondered how it would be possible to write again. The horror of that experience seemed to defy representation and to discredit the entire enterprise of Western culture. My argument in this book is that Findley fuses his attempt to make sense of the holocaust with his need, as a North American, to come to terms with the European colonization of the Americas and mistreatment of indigenous peoples. North Americans might feel tempted to see the holocaust as a European problem, but Findley sees parallels between the Nazi attempt to eliminate the Jewish people, the U.S. bombing of Hiroshima and Nagasaki, and the North American settlers' campaign to eradicate and assimilate North American Indians. For him, these issues are moral more than they are political, but in his first two books he is less concerned with probing the heart of evil than he is with addressing the dangerous complicities of innocence.

Whereas the literature of the United States has often mobilized the biblical myth of the Garden of Eden to celebrate the American citizen as a New World Adam, Canadian literature has traditionally focused on the darker side of this myth: the expulsion from the Garden and a deep awareness of original sin. Politically, this has led to very different forms of governance, with the Canadian constitution guaranteeing only "peace, order and good government" instead of the more flamboyant American promise of "life, liberty, and the pursuit of happiness." Canadians, then, have a literary tradition of suspicion around the notion of innocence. Therefore, after the news of the Nazi concentration camps were made public and the world disclaimed responsibility through protesting ignorance of what was really going on, Findley found himself wondering about the nature of innocence itself.

His first two novels take as their focal points of consciousness two innocent witnesses of their times whose observations record social hypocrisies and whose subsequent actions throw into question the nature of innocence. Hooker Winslow of *The Last of the Crazy People* is the innocent watcher, introduced in the framing prologue as awake all night in the knowledge of what he must do as a result of a summer of watching the adults around him. He unleashes a massacre that the novel explicitly presents as a symbolic version of holocaust. Ruth Damarosch is the innocent dreamer of *The Butterfly Plague;* the relation between Ruth's dreams and the novel's reality is ambiguously presented so that there is the clear possibility that she has unleashed at least some of the holocaustic fires that mirror the Nazi horrors in this novel.

The Final Solution: *The Last of The Crazy People*

The Last of the Crazy People, Findley's first novel, develops its thematics of complicity around three intersecting fields of reference: the connections of imperialism and fascism, of love and death, and of money and power. These are the ambivalences *The Last of the Crazy People* invokes and fails to resolve in its apocalyptic climax. In this novel, Findley's invocations of southern gothic writers (specifically Carson McCullers and Tennessee Williams), and his use of Oscar Wilde as a touchstone, draw connections between the pre-Civil War American South and Edwardian England through a shared focus on aristocratic style and the defining gesture. Canada is located somewhere between these American and British models. In following these models, *The Last of the Crazy People* locates self-conscious style rather than interiority as the marker of meaning. In other words, character is revealed to the reader through gestures, actions, and, to a lesser extent, dialogue, rather than through giving the reader access to a character's inner consciousness. Such a technique is indebted to the public style of Oscar Wilde.

Although early reviewers seemed puzzled by *The Last of the Crazy People,* contemporary critics have begun to see patterns of thematic focus and generic performance that link it to Findley's later texts. Lorraine York reads *Crazy People* as a novel of domestic war that deals with polarity and conflict within the family through invocations of the American Civil War as a domestic conflict between North and South on the national scale. At the level of the family, she sees the novel recording "the battle for the affections of the mother" (York, *Front Lines,* 12). This reading privileges the conflict between an older and younger brother, prefiguring the Bud and Neil stories of *Stones.* For Donna Pennee, the family is subordinate in interest to Hooker Winslow, whom she sees as "the prototype for a figure that remains central to Findley's fictions" (Pennee, *Moral,* 22). This figure is characterized by a sensitivity to the "incongruities between experience and knowledge, curious about the power of language to refer and to satisfactorily explain" (22), and prepared to act against ordained precedents when his or her own conscience dictates otherwise. Pennee draws attention to the contemporary context of the novel's setting: the Civil Rights movement of the 1960s (and its Civil War intertext) and the assassination of President Kennedy, which Hooker watches on television. Interestingly, Hooker identifies with Oswald, the assassin, against the dominant community interpretation of this traumatic event.

Barbara Gabriel's focus is generic. She argues that "this is a novel that *performs* Southern Gothic in an unusually flagrant way for its own time and place" (Gabriel, "Staging," 171). For her, "[I]t is the figure of the monstrous as *stigmatized body* that grounds homologies of *queerness, difference, imperfection,* and *madness* throughout Findley's fiction" (173), and this pattern is first revealed in *Crazy People.* Gabriel develops a complex argument connecting discourses of monstrosity and madness to the containment and policing of homosexual desire in modern history, beginning with the public trials of Oscar Wilde and running through the Nazi persecutions of homosexuals and the attacks of the McCarthy era, including the so-called " 'security' dismissals of gay men and women in the Canadian federal service in the late 1950s and 1960s" (184), the context (and pretext) for Findley's play *The Stillborn Lover.* Gabriel's reading sees the novel proceeding through a series of displacements and substitutions, addressing Hooker's sense of sexual difference, which cannot be expressed openly in such times of persecution, by appearing to focus on his parents' and his brother's inabilities to fulfill their prescribed gender roles, and on the marginalization forced on the family maid, Iris, because of her blackness.

These differently focused readings come together in their identifications of the ways in which Findley's account of the private life of a singular family intersects with public and social events. Making meaning, developing interpretations, and drawing conclusions are seen as socially determined as well as socially significant acts. My own focus in reading this text develops the insights of earlier critics to consider how the novel questions (but at crucial moments also seems to buy into) the notion of violence as a solution to difficulties. Through discussions around the kitchen table between Hooker, his brother, Gilbert, and Iris, the family maid, the novel surveys the range of justifications for violence, discussing the idea of a "crime of passion" as celebrated in the novel's signature song, "Frankie and Johnnie," and in its signature ballad, Oscar Wilde's "Ballad of Reading Gaol." At the opposite extreme of interpretation, these characters consider versions of "mercy killing" as developed through nineteenth-century eugenics, advocated by some North American settlers as a solution to their "Indian problem," and practiced in Nazi death camps as Hitler's "Final Solution." Through Alberta, Iris's friend, the novel introduces the notion of divine retribution and apocalypse, God's version of a love that kills. When Hooker asks Alberta what Armageddon means, she explains that it will be a day of mass death and horror but also "a glorious day of release" for the oppressed.[1] She introduces Hooker to the idea that death can be seen as liberating for those killed. Gilbert suggests to Hooker that it can also be liberating for those doing the killing. When Lee Harvey Oswald assassinates President Kennedy, Hooker asks Gilbert what "assassinate" means. Gilbert replies that it is "killing for a bigger reason than plain ordinary murder" (*Crazy,* 68) and speculates that "[h]e thought that if he killed the President, then he could be happy, one way or another. Free, if you like that better" (69).

Each discussion of murder in which Hooker participates sets up a different justificatory model. Hooker is encouraged by explanations that see death as a blissful release. Disturbingly, the novel endorses this view in its description of the final moments of the people Hooker murders. Hooker's father, Nicholas, is "thrown back into a violent stillness" (279), a description that aestheticizes his death as a modernist work of art. Hooker's mother, Jessica, is described as feeling her hands rise to her mouth "in a gesture of amazed release" (280). Her son has succeeded at last in alleviating her suffering. His aunt, Rosetta, in a simile that most powerfully suggests that she is responsible for her own death, falls "forward with the gesture of a Japanese Samurai who has committed hari-kari" (279). Each of these descriptions powerfully suggests that these deaths are not only warranted but positively welcomed.

Findley himself has endorsed such a reading of this novel, telling Cameron: "I think Hooker is a saviour figure" (Cameron, 51). He concludes: "We must destroy what is destroying us. We must kill what is killing us. We must violate the violators ..." (62). Such a statement seems meant to be taken symbolically rather than literally. Even so, it raises the problem of complicity. How is the violator who fights violation differentiated from the violator who perpetuates it, presumably for its own sake? Is intent sufficient separation between the murderer and the righteous executioner, and what authority confers the right to kill on some and not on others? These were questions raised by conscientious objectors to both world wars, and they carried sufficient force to convince Canadians to abolish the death penalty.

By focusing on how human beings use and rationalize violence, projecting fears of their own monstrosity onto stereotypes of various kinds of monstrous others in *Crazy People*, I have identified clear strands of concern linking this novel to Findley's other work. He returns obsessively to themes of betrayal and abandonment, visibility and invisibility, and the rewards and penalties afforded the performance and nonperformance of socially prescribed gender roles. The question that titles his first play, "can you see me yet?," and the complaint that titles his last novella, "you went away," both echo through the action of *Crazy People* as possible explanations for Hooker's decisive act. Everyone in his family is too preoccupied with their own concerns to pay attention to Hooker. As a virtually abandoned child, left to his own resources, he makes friends with his cats and the family maid. The lonely child and the notion of parental abandonment recur as motifs throughout Findley's fiction.

Although this is arguably the only text where the child's quest for visibility takes the form of killing, Findley returns regularly to the issue of whether or not taking another life can ever be justified. Several of Findley's characters decide that they have the moral authority and even the obligation to kill others for their own or for a greater good. Although I think that Hooker's act is ultimately presented as tragically misguided when viewed rationally, it is also presented as aesthetically and emotionally satisfying.

Through linking Hooker's massacre of his family to Hitler's identification of various social scapegoats that, once identified, can be annihilated, Findley suggests that a similar scapegoating strategy enabled the conquest and settling of Canada as an imperial colony. Because Hooker's family is dysfunctional, he eliminates its component parts, effectively killing the family to save the family. Findley's novel implies that the logic of fascism (and imperialism) works the same way: To save the state, they will destroy it, by progressively eliminating all of the elements they identify as threats to its ideal order. The absolutism, arrogance, and futility of seeking a "final solution" to the complexities of human life on this earth is anathema to Findley. But precisely because he finds this quest both abhorrent and fascinating, he needs to understand it. By refusing to label Hooker a monster, and by seeking instead to understand how he could come to see mass murder as a solution for civilization's discontents, Findley refuses the thinking in terms of absolutes that he believes has led to fascism in the first place.

In its echoing of Fenimore Cooper's *The Last of the Mohicans,* Findley's title, *The Last of the Crazy People,* invokes the public context of colonial genocide and its twentieth-century equivalent in the holocaust. But the analogy the novel draws between these public events of historical record and the private difficulties of the fictional Winslow family is slippery and inexact. The well-to-do but dysfunctional Winslow family cannot logically be compared to the First Nations resisting colonialism or to Jews and homosexuals stigmatized by the Nazis. The fact that the Winslows themselves sometimes draw such connections only seems to reinforce how out of touch they are. The fact that Findley's text seems to endorse these analogies suggests that an emotional logic is working against the intellectual elements of the story, rendering the book interesting to the critic but unsatisfying at a structural level despite its circular action and decisive sense of an ending. I suspect that settler-colonial guilt is being displaced from North America's history of broken contracts with the First Nations onto an abhorrence of the Nazis in *Crazy People*. The language of Auschwitz and Belsen resonates in the public mind in a way the Trail of Tears and Wounded Knee still do not. The treatment of native peoples in North America haunts the consciousness of all settler societies on the continent, but Canadian and American public culture did not begin to address that historical guilt openly until very recently. The implicit comparison drawn between the Winslows and First Nations through the title's echoing of Fenimore Cooper's book is politically inappropriate, and logically inexact, but emotionally compelling through the dynamic of unspoken guilt.

I am arguing that Findley did not have the language at the moment in history when he wrote his book to fully articulate the links he saw between imperialism and fascism and their scapegoating of others, but that he signaled these connections through his title. Postcolonial critics argue that "the great categories that came to define the modern age— race and citizenship, civility and authority, for example—were haunted, from the start, by the colonial question."[2] These are the categories that Findley's work recurrently explores. This colonial haunting is not particular to Canada, of course, but it takes a distinctively national form in Canada that Findley tentatively begins to explore in *Crazy People*. Here, through the story of a young boy trying to make sense of the contradictions he experiences between what he is told and what he senses, Findley explores the changing dynamics of power relations within the colonial context.

Despite the novel's apparent simplicity on one level, what happens in this text is actually very complicated. Set during a long, hot summer in a young boy's life, the novel records the process through which Hooker

Winslow, the 11-year-old protagonist, makes his own strange sense of his life, observing the deterioration of his parents' marriage and his brother's suicide, until he eventually decides that the only thing he can do to save them all is to kill his remaining family. The novel works hard to persuade its readers that, given the context in which Hooker finds himself, his conclusions are inevitable and carry their own fateful logic.

It opens with a prologue set during the family's final night, with Hooker watching and waiting the long night through, accompanied only by his cat, whose eyes echo the potential for explosion expressed in his own. With the stage set for some final explosion, the story moves back to the beginning of the summer. The body of the novel tells the story of the family's decline over their final few months through the voice of an omniscient narrator who is often confined to expressing Hooker's limited understanding of what is seen and heard, but who also ranges freely into the minds of the other characters from time to time. In the epilogue, the scene established in the prologue reaches its apparently inevitable conclusion.

My point here is that a deterministic view of events is built into this novel formally. Findley wants us to believe that this outcome was tragically predetermined, but he also wants us to see that *Crazy People* is more than just the story of a single family, that the Winslows are representative of a larger public reality. What happens to notions of human responsibility and agency when this structure of historical determinism is used to explain both personal and public history? The effect is to diminish readers' sense of Hooker's agency, but possibly to increase their own personal sense of agency. Findley's novel wishes to avoid a rhetoric of blame. He needs readers to understand that Hooker is close enough to them in humanity that they, too, in his circumstances, might have acted as he did. With that understanding in place, and with the larger perspective on Hooker's dilemma that the novel provides, readers can also see alternative courses of action that Hooker, caught within the text, is unable to see.

But the novel is not always able to negotiate this balance between identification with Hooker and distancing from him. The novel's narrative logic demands that the conclusion be seen as deeply satisfying. Hooker's killing spree in the final pages of the novel provides what Findley terms, in a revealing interview, "the blessed relief of action. It's almost like orgasm in a funny way. It's a terrible striving for a necessary climax without which we do go insane."[3] This sounds more like the writer talking about finishing a novel than about Hooker murdering his family, but the identification with the character here is very clear. At a personal level, a writer, especially a beginning writer, may need an excuse for killing off progenitors to clear a space for his own work. Nancy Huston argues that all writers need to kill off their parents to give birth to themselves, so that all novels effectively declare: "Look Ma, no navel."[4] This first novel may be read as Findley's own killing of the things he loves. In a massive clearing gesture, he provides himself with space to reinvent the world and a place for himself within it. Such a gesture clearly identifies him as working within a modernist tradition he has not yet begun to question. The influences of southern gothic writers and Oscar Wilde are written in so they can be written out.

In creating a story about a protagonist on the verge of adolescence who frees himself from the constraints of his family, the novelist vicariously frees himself of similar constraints. Hooker abolishes origins, just as the novelist wishes to declare himself original through denying his literary parentage. At the same time, in documenting Hooker's tragic story of misreading social cues and other narratives, Findley may be dramatizing his own fear of being misconstrued, and perhaps also a related fear of being read too well, of having his protective disguises penetrated and his cover blown.

For Hooker, the stakes are different. In wiping out his family, Hooker frees himself to begin again but at the cost of abdicating his place in the world as a "sane" member of the community. Hooker is freed from the trap of the family into the prison of the mental health care system, and at the end of the novel is incarcerated once more. Ironically, Hooker's sanity-making climax proves him insane in the eyes of the world. Findley suggests in the same interview that "[t]he ultimate sanity comes from the insane . . . we call the *sane* 'insane' " (Gibson, 122). This seems to be the inverted logic that drives the story of *Crazy People,* a logic popularized in the 1960s through the widespread acceptance of the psychological theories of R. D. Laing. It is a theory that Findley tests in most of his writing.

Yet this claustrophobic story of the decline of privilege in a well-to-do Canadian family fits uneasily with the political baggage Findley asks it to bear. The Winslows are characterized as the victims of historical change, yet it is hard to see this privileged family as without agency. The Winslows are depicted as out of place in twentieth-century North America, where the values of civility and authority that once made them seem superior now only serve to make them seem crazy. Findley tells Graeme Gibson that "the Winslow family, as individuals and collectively, represented a lot of values and things that must go. . . ." (134). He explains:

> In fact the particular situation in that book is peculiar to Canada. It doesn't exist anywhere else in the world, that kind of family. . . . Canada being the age it is, had a rise towards a power structure, a rise towards a kind of aristocracy at the turn of the century. War brought it down; we then became, after the First World War, a cultural eunuch; we were neither male nor female, but we had the propensity of feeling one thing and of being another. . . . The whole era left a residue of these people, it left a residue of Winslows, of lost people with nowhere to go and no essential background, except two generations before that they were farmers. (134)

Here Findley seems to be creating his own version of the noted Canadian propensity to sympathize with the underdog; the "beautiful losers" tradition immortalized in Leonard Cohen's novel of that name, and with the Canadian "tory myth," a view of Canadian history that privileges landed wealth and the values of a preindustrial world. Findley's sympathetic identification with these "lost" people, a class who gained wealth rapidly over a few generations and then lost it even more quickly, is signaled by the shift he makes in his interview with Gibson from talking about them in the third person to speaking of them in the first person plural, as "we," when he moves from describing their rise to wealth and influence, which he associates with his grandfather's generation, to noting their decline. In this sense, the novel can be read as an elegy for a lost way of life, written out of Findley's own sense of exile from the privilege of his family's past.

That Findley should designate this group decline as a neutering of sexuality is also interesting for understanding the links his fiction makes between sexuality, power, and desire in the Canadian context. The colonial mentality is often characterized as a kind of "colonial castration" or, as Northrop Frye puts it, a "frostbite at the roots of the imagination."[5] Hooker describes his family, after their "troubles," as "frozen" into postures from which they can't extricate themselves (*Crazy*, 12). Rosetta, the unmarried aunt, is described by Alberta as the "Deep Freeze" (90). When Hooker last visits his mother before conceiving his "dreadful thought" (271), he notes that she "seemed like a figure cut from ice, in the process of being melted" (270). The Winslow family condition is a colonial condition, a paralysis that results from trying to maintain outmoded patterns of privilege in a changing context.

Findley's title suggests that the Winslows' ethic of noblesse oblige, a mix of snobbery with values of decency, civility, and self-control, has become obsolete in the same way that nineteenth-century settlers believed that native peoples' mode of living on the land was becoming obsolete in the face of western settlement. The elegy for a lost way of life, whether transplanted British gentility or idealized noble savage, is a standard colonial genre. Findley's use of it here shows both its durability and its inherent weaknesses. Similarly, the explicit comparisons drawn between the situation of the Anglo-Saxon Winslow family in Canada and the Jews in Nazi Germany seem incongruous and inappropriate, unless one recognizes an emotional pattern of substitution that conflates homosexuals with Jews as both targets of the Nazi "final solution."

When Hooker's mother shows signs of mental instability and her son Gilbert is accused of impregnating a local debutante, Hooker's aunt, Rosetta, complains to his father, Nicholas: "This simply is not a normal quota of trouble at all. This is different. It's like being marked for something. Like the Jews at Auschwitz" (63). A little later, as he watches Hooker cart away a wounded squirrel maimed by one of his cats, Gilbert complains to Iris, the family's maid: "This is like living in Belsen" (77). Even Iris, listening to the family fight upstairs, suggests that "[t]his is like some kind of air raid" (152). And the narrator describes one of the cats as sporting "Hitler's moustache on a black-and-white countenance" (254). Perhaps the first two of these comments are designed to show the reader how out of touch with reality these Winslows are, yet the later examples suggest that they come with some authorial endorsement. Again, when Nicholas is asked if he knows the father of the young woman whom rumor says Gilbert got pregnant, he is described by the narrator as speaking "as he might if he had been asked, 'Do you know Adolf Hitler?' " (139). These incidents signal that *Crazy People* is trying to come to terms with culturally sanctioned forms of victimization, and to understand how human beings could come to a position where they could see genocide as a solution, but because the settler inheritance in Canada is so overdetermined, and because homosexuality carried such a stigma at the time this book appeared, the novel's way into these issues is blocked. Like the settler inheritance they represent, the Winslows are both victims and victimizers. Unable to cope with that double casting, they self-destruct.

The title of the novel refers in a general sense to the entire Winslow family, whom their friends, neighbors, and servant describe as crazy, and, more specifically, to the family's youngest son, the 11-year-old Hooker

Winslow, through whose consciousness most of the story is filtered. Hooker literally becomes the last of his doomed family after his older brother's suicide and his own choice to murder his father, mother, and aunt in a misguided act of mercy. Unlike the various victims of genocide that the novel presents as analogous to the Winslows, Hooker's family *chooses* to end their line before Hooker decides to kill them. Jessica Winslow, Hooker's mother, expresses her "craziness" through her refusal to bear any more babies. This refusal is precipitated by the stillbirth of a third son, who would have been named Patrick after the father's dead brother. With her decision, the family has reached a dead end. She will produce no more Winslows. Each of her sons decides, in his own way, that he will make the same decision. In refusing procreation, they refuse the fundamental tenet of heterosexuality as an ideology, but in the context of Findley's fictional world, they also refuse their responsibility to the continuity of life itself. That refusal makes them appear perverse and insane to people for whom these values are incontestable.

In her sorrow for the dead baby, Jessica turns against the living. She rejects her husband and children to retreat from the world entirely. In thinking about her defection, her husband, Nicholas, wonders about her identity: "Who was she? She was not the woman he had known and married—beautiful, sensitive, in some ways even fun, although never beyond the point of propriety. She had worn clothes well, and wealth. She had led the proper life for the wife of a Winslow" (38). The descent into bathos marks his failure of insight. He has never seen his wife as a full person but only her ability to fulfill the social role demanded of her as his wife. Nicholas sees her rejection of procreation as an aberrant personal decision. He cannot accept her accusation that his own failure to perform a suitably masculine role has led her to reject the prescribed female role of repeated motherhood. Neither seems comfortable with these prescribed gender roles, yet they are trapped by them.

Jessica mourns: "My men. My men. All my men. Hopeless failures. Everyone of them. Useless. Hopeless. Failures" (39). Her lament is echoed by Rosetta's thought, as she watches the impotent Nicholas: "I have been left without any men to take care of me" (154). Gilbert attacks Nicholas as an inadequate father, someone who is never there: "Aren't you my father? I'd like to know what kind of fucking father *you* had" (146). Hooker, observing that "[m]y father has hurt my mother" (52), concludes: "I'm never going to hurt a mother" (53). Later he adds, "It isn't fair that I have to marry a woman. . . . Mama shouldn't have been married at all" (54). The family's craziness, it seems, stems from their inability to live within the constrictions of prescribed gender roles.

Although Nicholas's sister, Rosetta, waits on her brother like a servant, she wields the authority that the outside world suggests should more properly remain the prerogative of the father. In its subliminal recalling of the Rosetta Stone, her name suggests the perversity of her position: the feminine fragility of the rose is frozen into the hardness of a rock, an indecipherable surface masking the emotions beneath. Her face, partially paralyzed by a stroke, reflects similar ambivalence. She is half dead, half alive. And while her stroke is the ostensible physical cause of this condition, the novel hints that the death of her suitor in the war is an equally important cause of her emotional frigidity. Her insistence on propriety and Nicholas's fear of being the target of gossip combine to force Gilbert's suicide.

This family has been damaged by history. The damage generated by the First World War can be articulated, and is represented through the photographs of the dead that dominate the Winslow and Harris houses and by the pistol that Hooker steals from the Harris household to protect Gilbert. After Gilbert's suicide, Hooker uses this pistol, a relic from the First World War, to murder the rest of his family. But the damage generated by colonialism, the text implies, cannot be so easily represented. The Winslows live trapped in the claustrophobia of their emotional needs and their mausoleum-like house. They are cut off from the land, from the lives of other people, from the history of their time and place. They are seen by Iris and Alberta, the black maids, as crazy, confirming society's outside view of this family. Iris says it is as if they are all asleep, sleepwalking through their lives, obsessed with the dead and oblivious to the living.

In some ways Iris and Alberta are stereotypes. Iris is close to the kindly black mammy figure of the white racist imagination, and Alberta is the fiery prophetess of biblical disaster. Both characters function as foil and complement to the Winslows, but they also exist beyond the Winslows' shadow as characters with their own histories and voices, who testify to a reality outside the claustrophobia of the Winslows' world. In their outsider relation to the white bourgeois family they function as powerful figures of desire. In the terms established by Toni Morrison in *Playing in the Dark*, they are "surrogate and enabl[ing]" figures.[6] Like the Winslows, Iris lives in the shadow of her dead, but her relation to death is valorized whereas theirs is deplored. Iris is a survivor. Implicitly, the novel recognizes that the Winslow's wealth is tied to their color through the declaration that Iris's family's poverty is tied to their color. The narrator comments: "Her mother believed in a graceful acceptance of her color. But she died. Iris' father believed only in the curse of his color. He lived longer. But not much. It was poverty really that killed them both—and all the others" (*Crazy,* 17). The Winslow's world depends on the labor of Iris and Alberta, but it also depends on their poverty. The economic and social order that decreed such relations is shifting, and bringing down the Winslow family with it. Hooker's half-comprehension of these changes and the novel's ambivalence about them create the tensions in a story that readers know must lead inexorably toward doom for the Winslows.

In chapter one, Iris and Hooker have an argument about identity and self-naming that brings racial, gender, and species categories together. Hooker wants to know why Iris calls herself Miss Iris Browne. Although Hooker's motivation for starting the conversation is unclear, his curiosity seems motivated by his own sexual uncertainties, and his need to understand the sexual designation signaled by the word "Miss" and the heterosexual hegemony it assumes. Iris's response, in contrast, is generated by her sensitivity to the possibility of a racial slur, and her consequent need to claim the recognition of human status signaled by the word "Miss." Such cross-purpose talk and misunderstanding characterizes the failure of community in the novel as a whole, and prepares the ground for Hooker's tragic misunderstanding of murder as a possible solution for family failure.

But this talk also signifies the novel's interest in categorization and in relations of sameness and difference. Hooker argues that "Iris" should be a sufficient naming, because Iris speaks "Negro" (20). Iris responds: " 'I got every right to my name. An' as for bein' a colored person—have you considered, Mister Hooker, how many other colored persons live in this town here? Lots,' she said. 'Lots of them and all of them with different names' " (20). Iris claims individuality and human status through insisting on the title "Miss Iris Browne." Later in the argument, blaming the question on Gilbert, Iris demands to know: " 'Where does he think we live—the States? *We* wasn't ever slaves, you know!' " (21). As the descendant of black Americans who came to Canada through the underground railway in flight from slavery, Iris claims a national identity and a history that distinguish her both from American blacks and from Canadian whites at the same time as she claims her right to full citizenship in the Canadian state. For Canadian readers, especially at the time this novel was first published in 1967, Iris's presence and words challenge a Canadian smugness that assumes, incorrectly, that race is not an issue for either the Canadian state or the Canadian novel.

The conversation seems to shift inconsequentially to a discussion of the relative merits of dogs and cats, yet this too bears on the question of categorization and identity. When Gilbert argues that dogs at least are human, Hooker, instead of disputing the claim, insists that "[c]ats are human, too" (24). Literally, this is nonsense; yet it shows a human need to define others as the same if we are to love them. Animals can only be admitted to the home when they are emotionally redefined as "human." Since Hooker's cats have already been described as efficient, compulsive, and gratuitous killers, his claiming of them here for the category of the human suggests that humans too are in some way natural killers. Findley also seems to be implying that cats adopted these habits through their association with humans. Barbarity and civilization are two sides of the same coin.

What does this have to do with Iris? In trying to map the boundaries between male and female, black and white, cat and human, Hooker has initiated this conversation in search of answers. He is dismayed to discover that Iris finds his question insulting and demeaning. Defined as "Negro" and therefore "other," Iris sees that she is being placed in a category apart from what is acknowledged as human in a dominant white society.

Gilbert, obsessed with the defeat of the South in the American Civil War, as if his own incapacity in life is somehow tied to that defeat, further goads Iris into an expression of resistance that Hooker and the reader can only partially grasp. "I'm reading *Lee's Lieutenants*. And you know what? I've been thinking. If the South—" Gilbert is interrupted by Iris's sigh, and then her response: "The South of *what*? Said Iris with practised stupidity. And something else that Hooker could not quite put his finger on. A practised something else" (25–26). Chapter one ends with Iris's performance of what Homi Bhabha terms the "sly civility" of a resistance to colonial power that mimics conformity while practicing dissent.[7] Hooker's uncertainty, and these lengthy, seemingly pointless conversations that imply more than they can say, create in the reader a sympathy for Hooker's acute sense of being left out of things, without the necessary key for unlocking the secrets of adult interactions.

That sense of mystery and unnamed horror, invoked in the foreboding scene set in the prologue and deepened through the conversations of the first chapter, can be seen as an adaptation of the gothic genre to the Canadian scene. When Graeme Gibson suggests to Findley that the atmosphere of the book could be called "southern Ontario Gothic" (Gibson, 138), Findley agrees, and elaborates: "[T]hat is it, the dead end of the Family Compact. It couldn't be better said, and those were the people I grew up with. And all the pretensions that have come out of that, which are tragic pretensions, and of course comical because it's tragic it's equally comical" (139). Findley's confused syntax mirrors the generic blurring of tragic and comic that marks his perception of this period of Canadian history. The Family Compact was a term used in 1828 by reformers in Upper Canada (now Ontario) to designate "the ultra conservative group that controlled policy and patronage" in the colony.[8] Findley's ambivalence about the demise of inherited privilege and the reconstitution of power through renewed closed circles of powerful people mixes nostalgia with anger as he mourns what has been lost and castigates their replacements.

If *Crazy People* mourns the decline of people like the Winslows, then *Headhunter* reserves its fury for those who have replaced them in the new social order of the late twentieth century: the *nouveau riche*. "The Group of Men" is a new Family Compact with all the greed and none of the civility of the old. Findley's anger at both groups of men stems from his conviction that patriarchal privilege is responsible for most of the sufferings in the world. In *Inside Memory*, Findley justifies his inclusion of the rape scene in *The Wars* because he believes it is essential to show that "[i]t has to be there because it is my belief that Robert Ross and his generation of young men were raped, in effect, by the people who made that war. Basically, their fathers did it to them" (*Memory*, 151). As Tom Hastings argues, this is a refrain that echoes through all of Findley's books, beginning with *Crazy People*, where the narrative implies that Hooker's Armageddon symbolically repeats the violence done to him by his father and his grandfather's generation. Hooker's massacre, then, can be seen as the equivalent of Robert murdering his commanding officer in *The Wars* in his effort to save the horses: a shocking scene of violence that dramatizes an uncomfortable recognition that human beings cannot help being complicitous in the very things they most deplore. Hooker decides to kill after he has been violated by Findley's notion of "the fathers"; not his biological father, as Tom Hastings explains, but older men who symbolize through their actions the ways in which the older generation has betrayed the trust of the younger.

Findley self-consciously draws attention to the political functions of gothic conventions in *Crazy People* through the disagreement between Iris and Gilbert about how to interpret Iris's favorite song, "Frankie and

Johnnie." Gilbert thinks it is a murder story, but Iris argues that it is a love story (*Crazy*, 42). *Crazy People* creates similar generic instabilities. Findley speaks of a true story that parallels his fictional story in *Crazy People*, in which the child murderer, when asked why he did it, responds, "Because I loved them so" (Gibson, 136). When Iris explains that "Frankie and Johnnie" is a Canadian love story, Gilbert contradicts her: "Nobody kills someone they love" (*Crazy*, 45). But inwardly, he knows she is right. He remembers the lines of the Oscar Wilde ballad and thinks: "Oscar Wilde was queer. Frankie was a spade. The world was made of strangeness, madness, and fear. And the weirdest people found each other in love" (46). Gilbert cannot allow himself to agree openly with Iris, his conversational antagonist, but his entire life seems dedicated to proving the truth of the ballad's assertion that "each man kills the thing he loves."

The allusive weight of literary and social history carried by the name "Oscar Wilde" is not spelled out but rather invoked in indirect ways in *Crazy People*. Oscar Wilde appears in almost every Findley text, operating as kind of shorthand for what Jonathan Dollimore calls an "aesthetic of transgressive desire," and for a demystification of "the normative ideologies regulating subjectivity, desire, and the aesthetic."[9] But Wilde's ideas, important as they are in their early advocacy of notions now associated with postmodernism, have been overshadowed by the image of Wilde's life as a performance of those ideas. He becomes an exemplary figure marking the transition between the nineteenth and twentieth centuries: a martyr and a figure of desire. As Dollimore argues, Wilde's ideas cost him his life: "One of the many reasons why people were terrified by Wilde was because of a perceived connection between his aesthetic transgression and his sexual transgression" (Dollimore, 67). In *Crazy People*, Gilbert also is accused of aesthetic transgression (plagiarizing his ballad) and sexual transgression (impregnating Janice Parker) in a way that connects him to Oscar Wilde and prepares the reader for his crucifixion-like self-sacrifice through suicide. Gilbert insists that both of the accusations against him are false; he wrote the poem and he did not impregnate the girl. Yet in a strange sense it is his innocence that seems most to infuriate his accusers. In this society men should not be writing poems and they should be impregnating women to prove their masculinity in socially acceptable terms. Whereas Nicholas, the father, is defined by his obedience to the edicts of society ("To the edict that in society we must do something to belong. To the edict of continuity, generation to generation" [*Crazy*, 147]), Gilbert's life is a dramatic gesture of refusal: he refuses bourgeois conformity, heterosexual norms, and polite decorum.

He refuses to apologize in the classroom, preferring to stage a scene and leave. Something similar occurs at the country club, when he openly challenges his family to accuse him of fathering Janice Parker's child, and then crashes his Jaguar through the trees to stage his fiery death. Hooker, too, will come to define his life through a single, misguided gesture, just as Wilde is remembered for the miscalculation of performance that doomed him at his trial. Both Gilbert and Hooker follow in the Wildean tradition of preferring an individualized gesture of refusal, however self-destructive, to collective political action for social change.

Findley describes Hooker's ordeal of growing up in *Crazy People* as the nightmare of "the ultimate arrival at adult life" (*Memory*, 74). Gilbert wants to spare Hooker this arrival, but cannot. As Hooker leaves the drugstore where he has had a milkshake, a "crazy" thing happens to him: "[H]e was touched, exactly as though he had been naked, in the soft part of the groin. Fingers, from somewhere, groped immediately and completely—and were gone" (*Crazy*, 183). Hooker does not know what to do about this violation. When he finally tells Gilbert, Gilbert's response is to sympathize with Hooker but also to identify with the old man who had touched him. His reply suggests that the man and Hooker are somehow complicit in this violation: " 'He had an impulse to touch you and you didn't stop him. Now. That's all right. But you see . . . some of us . . . ' He paused and then yelled out at the house: ' . . . WANT TO BE STOPPED!' " (196). This incident prompts him to tell the story of the ballad he wrote at school, for which he is expelled when he refuses to admit the teacher's charge that he has stolen it from a book. The emotional logic connecting these apparently disparate events is the shared theme of betrayal.

To trust an adult is to court betrayal. Adults cannot be trusted. In advocating this distrust of an older generation, the novel may seem to be appealing to the slogan of the youth movement of the baby boomer 1960s, "You can't trust anyone over 30," yet in its constant reminders of the Canadian boys who failed to return from the First World War, it draws as well on the mythology of generational conflict popularized by the British war poets. In Findley's fiction, however, this rhetoric of blame is complicated by an exploration of the ways in which the violated have been complicit in their own betrayal. Gilbert describes his resistance to his teacher's views as imagination holding out against "blind obedience to fact." What Gilbert's teacher wanted to destroy was his sense of "wonderment" (198). Gilbert intuits that Hooker's wonderment has drawn the old man's assault as a similar violation of specialness. In pondering the incident, Hooker thinks: "He knew, too, that he was different and that his own particular and private inquisitiveness— that was what made him so. . . . His mind, moving like the man's fingers over things in his imagination—this could betray him" (216).

This betrayal is felt viscerally, through the body and the mind. In the locker room at the club, Hooker realizes that his attitude to nakedness has changed as a result of his disorienting experience. The drugstore experience has made nakedness menacing. He thinks: "It was because, as a stranger, this man had known something about Hooker that Hooker did not know about himself. About himself. Something dangerous. . . . It was like a secret communication from a club. Something in code. A question. Or an answer" (216). Hooker fears that it is something about himself that has drawn this man to him and decides not to risk showering at the club. A later encounter with a friend of his father's is charged with an uncomfortable eroticism, a sense of exposure, and a fear of ridicule.

Hooker and Gilbert are linked in their alienation from the world of normative behavior, Gilbert through a loathing that comes from knowledge and Hooker from a fear that comes from incomprehension. Gilbert suggests that there are many different stories that could be told about who they are. One version says they are crazy. Another says that they are "civilized" and "aristocrats" (201). These words for their difference link them to the transgressive style of an Oscar Wilde, suggesting a contempt for the normative masculinity and middle-class lifestyle promoted through the school and the country club, but a contempt that is based on outmoded notions of class privilege, dooming those who hold such beliefs to obsolescence.

The country club, where Hooker experiences shame about his own naked body and fear of the gaze and touch of older men, is importantly a place of privilege and wealth. It is where Gilbert chooses to stage his death, and where after his death, Hooker returns to the shower room, strips off his clothes and waits, "wishing somebody would come" (232). Is Hooker seeking to imitate Gilbert by staging a comparable act of self-immolation, acting out his own desire for extinction, or simply a quest for some human contact after the terror of death? The family craziness has now been made officially public (later to be ratified legally in the judgment of the inquest). There is nothing more to hide.

Gilbert is especially drawn to the work of F. Scott Fitzgerald, one of the most glamorous American writers of the so-called "Lost Generation," reading a personal significance into Fitzgerald's famous story

"The Crack-Up." Gilbert's drinking and his self-destructive behavior imitate the version of the writer's life popularized by Fitzgerald, who also documents North Americans' love/hate relationship with wealth, and the combined fascination and denigration that money arouses in its observers.

The Last of the Crazy People suggests that the Winslow family's craziness is tied to their wealth. By making them different from other people, their wealth marks them as potential scapegoats, should they show any weakness. In losing their money, they lose their protection. From being objects of desire, they become outcasts, people to be reviled. By showing events through Hooker's eyes, Findley suggests that the rich are at the mercy of their servants. When he goes to the store, Hooker feels attacked and victimized by the boy his own age who works there, although Hooker himself does not need to work for a living. Hooker's only confidante is his black maid. Although she nurtures him, she has a life of her own beyond her relationship with him. He does not. These relationships present Hooker as the cliché of the poor little rich boy. The rich are presented as special people, to be admired and pitied, but also as a species whose day has passed, mowed down by the growth of democracy. Findley is nostalgic for their passing even as he records their demise as inevitable. As Hooker looks at the family photographs after the inquest into Gilbert's death, "[H]e could see that there was a different code of ethics and behavior, different to the one he knew on the street today" (255). These ancestors represent ownership in the double sense of taking responsibility for one's life and accumulating possessions, but all Hooker's father and aunt can do is hoard memories and husband what little money is left from the fortunes once made. Gilbert seems to accuse his family not only of taking the wealthy Mr. "Railroad" Parker's side against him in the dispute over who made Janice Parker pregnant but also of failing to pass on to him the wealth they themselves had inherited (140–43). Gilbert is both paralyzed by the inheritance of tradition passed on to him by his family and disinherited of the wealth he feels rightly should belong to him. With the novel's implicit endorsement, he blames the father.

Just as the Winslows live on the border between the very rich and the merely rich, so their house is situated halfway between city and country. Hooker shoots his family from the security of the barn, and buries the birds, mice, and squirrels killed by his cats, and the corpse of the cat Clementine killed by his brother, in the field nearby. (The field, a symbolic space of great power in *Crazy People*, takes on even greater significance in *The Piano Man's Daughter*, where once again it becomes a place associated with the natural rhythms of life and death and the country's heritage in farming.) In *Crazy People,* Hooker uses the field as a cemetery, yet it is the one place in the novel teeming with life. When Hooker is forced to kill the squirrel to put it out of its misery after molestation by the cat, he watches two dragonflies mating, without comprehending what they are doing, on the very edge of the grave (79). After burying Clementine, he opens his ears to hear "the loud and perfected cry of all living things, spilling out in motion . . ." (164). Here in the natural world Hooker finds his only solace from the confusion and threat of his life. A green world of utopian dimensions, it is also a graveyard. Through symbolic displacement, this characterization of the field recognizes Canada's violent colonial past, rejecting the imperialist view of the land as a tabula rasa, an empty slate, and insisting that white Canadians must come to terms with their violent heritage before they can move forward. The implied audience of the book is white, as the characterization of Iris makes clear.

Iris comes to Hooker's field at the very end of the book, after Hooker has fulfilled his destiny and disappeared into the mental hospital. In a moment that seems to predict Mrs. Noyes's refusal to pray at the end of *Not Wanted on the Voyage,* Iris feels "an impotent wish for prayer" (281), but instead begins to sing "Frankie and Johnnie," an American *liebestod,* a song acknowledging the interconnectedness of love and death, and a song she has claimed for her own place and people. Iris walks out of the story and out of the field "in the direction of a journey of her own" (282). The final words of the book affirm: "The field and its welcome would always be there."

Barbara Gabriel argues that "the iconography of this scene establishes it within the mythos of the eternal return, erasing the violence inscribed within a teleological framework of life and death by reframing it within the play of sameness and difference—the 'changing of the season' " (Gabriel, "Staging," 193). Furthermore, she sees Findley appropriating the black figure of Iris to stand in for his own sense of difference. Without wishing to deny the validity of this reading, I want to complicate it further. Despite the way in which Iris recalls the symbolic figure of endurance conjured up by the white imagination to serve its own needs and immortalized in Faulkner's Dilsey of *The Sound and the Fury,* Iris can also be read in this scene as representing a new generation of Canadians, moving on and away from the Winslows but carrying the memory of their passing with her into a multicultural future. The field itself, though obviously meant to represent the natural world in a generalized sense, also stands for Canadian land; that is, land taken from native peoples and never really owned, in any true sense, by the Winslows. Hooker's field has its counterpart in the country club golf course. Described as a "typically Canadian view. Trees, grass, and distance" (*Crazy*, 214), the golf course is where Gilbert stages his death. By calling the novel *The Last of the Crazy People* and by peopling the land with the Winslows' dead bodies, Findley seems to be claiming this space as his heritage. The text appears to acknowledge difference (the natural world, Iris's presence) in order to incorporate it. This is a classic colonial literary move, memorably summarized in a long poem called "The Pride" by Findley's contemporary, John Newlove, in which the prior history of native peoples is assimilated into a white Canadian present so that the descendants of settlers may be freed to claim the Indians as their ancestors. In 1967, the year of Canada's centenary celebrations, this was a popular and publicly unquestioned kind of patriotic gesture for a white writer to make.

"The Voice of the Prophets"

The Butterfly Plague, first published in 1969, marks an astonishing stylistic shift but a continuity of interest in the dynamics of innocence and complicity in Findley's writing. This is a brilliant and insufficiently analyzed novel. Feeling that this was a book he had to write but that he had written too soon, Findley published the revised version 17 years later, in 1986. An unusual step for a writer to take, it suggests that the book means a great deal to him. In *Inside Memory* Findley reveals that the model for the fictional Ruth Damarosch was a close personal friend named Janet Baldwin, one of the four friends to whom the novel is dedicated. Through Ruth, he creates what he describes as an "innocent watcher" for an "exploration of evil" (*Memory*, 107–8). Such a description links Ruth to *The Last of the Crazy People*'s Hooker. Hooker's innocent eyes reveal the hypocrisies of family life. Ruth witnesses, and her story connects, some of the most decisive events of the twentieth century: Nazi concentration camps, the Berlin Olympics, the rise of Hollywood as entertainment capital of the world. Nonetheless, at the heart of her story lies a critique of the heterosexual nuclear family, which is perceived as inherently dysfunctional.

The novel records the interlinked stories of three families who live in Topanga Beach, California. Their stories are revealed in fragmented form, through a series of "chronicles," but the sequence the reader can piece together when the conclusion of the story has been reached looks something like the following. In 1904, George Damarosch, the film producer, had married Naomi Nola, whom he made into a silent film star. They had two children: Adolphus, called "Dolly," a film director and secret collector of pornography, and Ruth, a champion swimmer who married her Nazi coach, Bruno Haddon. George divorced Naomi when he discovered, during Ruth's 15th birthday party in 1922, that his son had hemophilia and his wife was a carrier. Ruth was traumatized by this rejection from her father. After banishing his family, George murdered Ping Sam, a Chinese-American working on the estate, in an incident described as "one of those scandals of silence" (*Plague,* 260). As George relives the scene in memory toward the end of his own life, he recalls moving toward the gardener, marching "like an army" (341). The narrator had earlier suggested that "[p]erhaps for George the basic problem was that he should have been a dictator" (171). These descriptions link George's violent temper and abuses of patriarchal privilege within the Damarosch family to the public abuses of power under the Nazis.

At the time the novel opens, in 1938, George and Naomi have been divorced for some time, Naomi is dying of cancer, Ruth has left Bruno to return home to her mother, and Dolly is making a film called "Hell's Babies" with Myra Jacobs in the starring role. In the course of the narrative, Myra, fighting a losing battle with fat that destroys her self-esteem, takes her own life. Her desperate telephone call to Dolly for help goes unanswered. Dolly bleeds to death in a car accident after witnessing a baseball star's murderous attack on a crowd of butterflies that the athlete sees as surrogates for the homosexuals he hates. After Dolly's death, Ruth discovers the pornography he has hidden in his collection of children's books (an image for how even the place of innocence has been defiled) and sets his house on fire in a scene of "holocaust" (327) as ritual cleansing.

Ruth seems to be experiencing a nervous breakdown. Her husband, Bruno, has subjected her to medical experiments in human endurance conducted in a Nazi concentration camp. Bruno's brutality is mirrored in the behavior of the high-ranking Nazi married to Ruth's school friend Lisa (now called Lissl). Lisa's home is bugged. Her servants are her jailers. Lisa's situation seems to justify Ruth's growing paranoia. Ruth imagines that she is followed by a mysterious man who "could have been an advertisement for racial perfection" (10). She associates him with the concept of "Race," an idea she fears but to which she is also fatally attracted, and one which she personifies. Ruth "dreams" her rape by this man, an ensuing pregnancy, and a repetition of the holocaust with animals as victims in the reserve called Alvarez Canyon. Naomi dies of the cancer, and George is violently dismembered by a car immediately after he shoots and kills the silent film star Letitia Virden at her comeback premiere.

Letitia Virden, the silent film star named "The Little Virgin," had blasphemously betrayed her bankbook image by secretly having an affair, presumably consummated the day of Ruth's 15th birthday party, and giving birth to a child 16 years before the narrative begins. Although the father of the child is not known, clues hint that he is the silent film dancing star Bully Moxon, who dances to his grisly death in front of Letitia and Ruth's train in the novel's opening chapter. Letitia had abandoned her son, her lover, and her career to flee the country immediately after the child's birth, but she has continued to provide financial support and as the novel begins is returning home to seek a reconciliation with him and to relaunch her career with the help of the millionaire financier of movies and armaments Cooper Carter.

Letitia's son, Octavius Rivi, lives in a beautiful house at the other end of the beach from Naomi. He is reclusive, living vicariously through the movies and the bizarre and regular ritual he performs in which he dresses himself as a woman, becoming the "Mother" he has never known. Watching old footage of Letitia, he notes the resemblance to his own masquerade and realizes that she must be his mother. He attends her comeback premiere dressed as "the Little Virgin," causing confusion and generating a new Hollywood legend through the doubled image he provides. Octavius had become friends with Ruth after they jointly witnessed Dolly's violently bloody death. The story of each reflects that of the other. He has been abandoned by his mother; she has been abandoned by her father. Each longs masochistically for a strong parental figure, each lives primarily through dreams, and each assumes the identity of "mother," Octavius through transvestism and Ruth through assuming her own mother's name, "Mrs. Damarosch." "I shall henceforth be Mrs. Damarosch," she tells her mother's nurse, Miss Bonkers, who thinks angrily: "Mrs Damarosch . . . is the mother's name" (234). When Octavius writes to Ruth at the end of the novel, informing her that he has fled to a new life with the first person he has ever loved, the Negro chauffeur he had first seen when he hired him for the premiere, we see the other side of Ruth's "beautiful" and "awful" dream of desire through the fulfilment of "Race" (41). Disturbingly, the narrator not only seems to share but actually seems to dwell on the fetishistic fascination these two characters feel for the bodies of these racial others: the blond perfection of the Nazi and the black mystery of the Negro (as African-Americans were described in this period).

The third family, comprising the sculptor Noah Telford, his wife, B. J., and their brood of eight children, functions as a foil of heterosexual normality to the tragically interlinked families of George Damarosch and Letitia Virden. Like George, Noah is an overbearing tyrant who makes his family suffer for his art and who puts the satisfaction of his own selfish needs above theirs. Their torture is posing for his monumental sculpture, "The Children's Crusade." Although Lorraine York sees the Telfords as providing positive images of fertility and acceptance of nature's ways, I see a more sinister quality in the words of Noah Telford that she quotes with approval: "Nothing is sad that's as it ought to be" (York, *Front Lines,* 65). Where York sees a resolution of life and death, I hear a smug complacency that is chilling in its lack of imagination and empathy for the plight of the butterflies. Noah assumes that his wife and children exist to serve him and that this convenient arrangement is "as it ought to be." This Noah seems to be a precursor of the more fully developed Noah in *Not Wanted on the Voyage.*

These overbearing fathers and Bruno, the father-husband, are the products of the same patriarchal society that has created a God whom Dolly describes as "just a wretched, sadistic old tyrant sitting up there inflicting diseases on innocent people" (*Plague,* 7). (Findley further develops this vision of God in *Not Wanted on the Voyage.*) In *The Butterfly Plague,* despite such throwaway observations, the focus falls on human tyrannies, as perceived and experienced through the innocent watcher and unreliable dreamer, Ruth.

Although Ruth is 31 years old when the novel begins, she holds onto innocence "like a renegade child" (10). That illusion of innocence allows her to maintain a tenuous hold on her sanity because to recognize her own part in the violence she is fleeing is too painful for her. Fleeing Nazi Germany and a brutally abusive husband for the California she calls home, she believes that she is "living in a nightmare," seeing darkness "when all around her the adults were proclaiming light" (10). Like Cassandra in *Can You See Me Yet?,* Ruth is the prophet whose warnings of pending disaster go unheeded.

The language of prophecy and doom seems the clearest link between these three early texts. Just as Hooker can see no logical reason for the cursed craziness of his family in particular, and Cassandra echoes the doomed voice of prophecy celebrated in Greek mythology, so the language of biblical plague in *The Butterfly Plague* suggests that the family's fate results from a divinely ordained punishment rather than from the choices they have made. Ruth's brother Adolphus says, only half playfully, "We are born to be driven mad at the whim of fate!" (7). Such imagery implicitly denies rather than claims cultural responsibility for the devastation of the Nazi regime, moving an account of fascist atrocities from the realm of the political into that of the moral. Findley clearly wishes his readers to share in Ruth's witnessing, but her difficulty in coming to terms with her complicity becomes a difficulty for the novel as a whole. The novel's narrator, like the character, affirms the validity of Ruth's perceptions. This validation, not just of the power but also of the truth of Ruth's nightmares, interferes with the novel's ability to negotiate between what is personal to Ruth as a character (her masochism and her visionary powers that make her seem mad or self-indulgent to those around her) and what is culturally shared with her society and her historical moment (her obsession with perfection and her firsthand experience of the Nazi concentration camps).

The mixture of attraction and repulsion that Ruth feels for Race is similar to the masochistic emotions experienced by Hugh Selwyn Mauberley for his Nazi murderer Reinhardt in *Famous Last Words*. Although Race seems to be sighted by other people and his distinctive scent of leather is smelled by his one blind victim, and although he seems to be responsible for an outbreak of violent rapes, murders, and fires that coincide with the butterfly plague, Ruth has apparently conjured this creature and his violent acts out of her own troubled negotiations with her personal desires, fears, and self-hatreds. Findley has developed this Conradian theme of secret sharing most extensively and powerfully in the short story "Dreams" from the collection *Stones*. There too the dividing lines between nightmare and reality, violator and violated, are abolished in a terrifying allegory for the monstrosity that Findley believes lies within every human being. The danger with such imagery, of course, is that it can seem perilously close to blaming the victim for having somehow willed victimization upon herself. (Similarly, when Myra stops fighting the New York men's vision of her as nothing but "Old Fat," her collapse is seen as a failure of will *and* as the natural process of aging {216–17}. She seems to be damned with the double whammy of having to assume blame for a personal failure and having to yield to her biological fate.)

By making Ruth, like his friend Janet on whom she is based, a carrier of hemophilia, Findley continues the debate about the ethics of bringing children into this world that he began in *The Last of the Crazy People,* but links it here to the Nazi obsession with breeding a perfect race through the science of eugenics. Just as the links he draws between the doomed Winslow family and the Jewish victims of the Nazi terror seem inappropriate in *The Last of the Crazy People,* so the links he draws in *The Butterfly Plague* between the doomed Damarosch family (who are part Jewish but whose doom is linked not to race but to hemophilia) and the Jewish victims of the holocaust also seem forced and unworkable through the confusions they suggest between what is natural and what is societal.

Ruth tells Octavius that she "met a dead man once," a Mr. Seuss who "carried his death with him in his pocket" in the form of a star (assigned to Jewish people by the Nazis as a marker of their difference). She continues: "The condemned, you see? Born that way" (352). When Octavius concludes, "Like Adolphus," she agrees, and goes on to extend the linkage: "Adolphus . . . Mr. Seuss . . . the butterflies . . . these other people—it's in their pocket. It's in their blood. It's with them all the time" (352). The text seems to endorse (or fails to distance itself sufficiently from) these careless equations that Ruth draws between socially assigned markers of difference, such as the notorious Nazi stars (also assigned in a different color to homosexuals), and diseases that are genetically carried from one generation to the next. Indeed, her metaphors seem to accept Nazi equations of Jewish heritage or homosexual lifestyle with biological disease. (Even Findley's wordplay encourages such associations, such as when he has Myra tease Adolphus by pretending to confuse the words homosexual and hemophilia by creating the composite word "homo-feely" [8], although when George later repeats this linguistic association it functions as a clear sign of his bigotry: "My son's a hemo-homo and now my daughter's a lesbian" [198]).

Ruth includes the butterflies in this associative train of connections, presumably because by their very existence in unusual numbers they have been labeled as a plague, and thus marked for killing, when their only drive is for life. Their urge "to be" is a drive Findley celebrates throughout his work. Findley clearly feels a strong personal identification with the monarch butterflies that invade and bring out the murderous instincts in the inhabitants of the novel's world. In the 25 November 1993 issue of the Fashion and Design section of the Toronto *Globe and Mail,* Canada's national newspaper, there is a photograph of Findley posed as a monarch butterfly (with the neck pulled over his face so that only his eyes are revealed and with his arms spread in flight).[10] In this regular celebrity feature entitled "My Favourite Object," Findley demonstrates the butterfly poncho created to celebrate the release of this novel that was knit for him by his partner William Whitehead, a biologist who specializes in insects as well as a writer. Nonetheless, although Findley values the butterflies as living creatures who contribute to nature's diversity, in the context of Nazi denigration of the humanity of their victims, it seems insensitive to compare Jewish people such as Mr. Seuss or hemophiliacs such as Adolphus to creatures most of the world sees simply as insects, and therefore as inherently less than human. Findley's point, however, is that reverence for life must be extended to all if it is to exist for humans.

In *The Butterfly Plague* Findley sees civilization itself as the plague that is destroying humanity. Ruth's comments obliquely identify the othering process by which civilizations define themselves through contrasts drawn between "them" and "us" as the problem that links the dreams manufactured in Hollywood with the Nazi dream of a purified race, and her reference to carrying one's heritage in one's pocket may reinforce this equation for the careful reader who remembers that Ruth herself carries two markers of her own fate in her pocket: the yellow star given to her by Mr. Seuss and the swastika given to her by the figure of Race in Alvarez Canyon. In Findley's fictional world, even the innocent are complicit, and the capacity for violence lies within everyone from birth. The disturbing opening image of the novel, a child's assassination of "Mickey Balloon," parodically repeats Hooker's assassinations from the end of *The Last of the Crazy People* as if to begin the novel with the reminder that the innocence normally associated with children includes the capacity to murder. Findley repeats this disturbing reminder in the blackly comic story of Charity Telford's "murder" of her invisible friend when his empty chair attracts the worried attention and then the punishment of her mother, B. J., the third mother on Topanga Beach. Nonetheless, the imagery here is muddied. Findley clarifies the imagery in his later novel *Headhunter,* where it is clear that the birds and dogs are not responsible for the sturnusemia plague that is blamed on them. In *The Butterfly Plague,* Dolly blames victims for their victimization, telling Ruth: " 'Victims are victims, by choice. Other people's choice first, and then their own' " (*Plague,* 296). Although Ruth rejects this interpretation as "[d]rivel," Dolly repeats the idea later to himself: "You die when you can't be real . . . When you can't see who you are and when you cannot see what is" (303). The conditions of Myra's death seem to confirm this pessimistic analysis.

Findley prefaces both versions of *The Butterfly Plague* with part of a poem by Nelly Sachs that urges readers to pay attention to the suffering around them:

> would you hear?
> If the voice of the prophets blew
> on flutes made of murdered children's bones—(n.p.)

The poem asks what is required to gain the attention and action of people to remedy social wrongs. This challenge to readers to "pay attention" recurs throughout Findley's work.

Sadly, *The Butterfly Plague*, despite its two versions and its melodramatic mix of sex and violence, has inspired very little critical commentary. The difficulty in making sense of this novel seems due to the instability and unreliability of Ruth Damarosch as a filtering consciousness (who speaks one chronicle in the first person) in combination with the ambition of its historical and geographical range, which goes from the 1920s to the 1940s and moves between Nazi Germany and Hollywood, and the mixed range of symbolisms these inspire. The present of the novel covers a brief time span, from August 1938, when Ruth and Letitia Virden return to California on the same train after prolonged absences, until April 1939, when Ruth is left the sole surviving member of her family and Octavius, Letitia's son, remains the sole surviving member of his family. This period of less than a year is the time span of the unusual natural occurrence labeled "the Butterfly Plague." However, the narrative ranges much more widely through time and space, moving between California and Germany to record Ruth's childhood and failed marriage to Bruno Haddon, and unveiling its action through flashbacks, memories, nightmares, visions, doubled stories of various kinds, and intertextual references to films of the period.

Just as *The Last of the Crazy People* appeared to confuse standard genre distinctions between bildungsroman, gothic, love, and murder stories, so *The Butterfly Plague* mixes a variety of narrative styles with chronicle. As a way of recording history, chronicles privilege the description of events over the analysis of cause and effect. A list of the chronicles that compose *The Butterfly Plague* gives a good overview of the dimensions of the book. The chronicle titles privilege character, time, and place, and taken together they create a sense of fragmentation. Instead of a continuous movement through a storyline, there are a series of apparently isolated stories that can be eventually pieced together through family connections but that remain essentially discrete. The chronicle titles fall into two categories: they are named for concrete elements, such as characters, places, or movies, or for abstract elements that reference human emotional and intellectual creations, such as nightmare, wish, or the concept of Race. Through naming, these titles seek to ground the narrative in concrete realities of time and place, providing the reader bewildered by the array of characters and the unclear links between them with some guidance through this labyrinth.

Barbara Gabriel describes *The Butterfly Plague* as "an unstable narrative of shifting genders and genres—its cross-dressed and sadomasochistic choreographies framed by a narrative in which transvestite camp uneasily confronts realist bildungsroman" (Gabriel, "Staging," 193). The cheek-by-jowl occurrences of black comedy, farce, bathos, and tragedy seem to be the novelist's way of approximating the unspeakable that the Nazi regime revealed at the heart of Western civilization, but they also claim the right to tell the old stories from a "queered" perspective. Concentration camps meet "camp," or "queer parody." Findley's use of camp seems best defined by Moe Meyer's insistence that camp is more than a style or sensibility; "it embodies a specifically queer cultural critique."[11] He defines "queer" as a term that challenges "dominant labelling philosophies, especially the medicalization of the subject implied by the word 'homosexual' . . . [and] discrete gender categories embedded in the divided phrase 'gay and lesbian' " (2). "Camp," then, is defined as "the total body of performative practices and strategies used to enact a queer identity, with enactment defined as the production of social visibility" (5). Findley's camp produces a kind of social visibility, but, as I have suggested, only ambivalently challenges the medicalization of same-sex desire, and sometimes risks reinforcing discrete gender categories.

The deployment of the camp chronicle of "The Little Virgin" and her androgynous and outrageous son is a good example of a narrative that might seem to be arguing against biological definitions of sexual identity in stressing the performance of gendered roles and in celebrating the son's difference. At the same time, the text punishes Letitia for failing to conform to the gender stereotypes of either the virgin (her performed role) or the mother (her biological role). The blasphemous parody of the cult of the Virgin Mary declares no sacred story sacrosanct. Findley reverses the biblical story of the annunciation so that the Little Virgin, in the role of the distant God the Father, sends the announcement not of the birth of Christ but of her own "rebirth" via the appropriately named Negro "angel," the chauffeur Harold Herald, to her son Octavius. This kind of exuberant play in disrupting tradition and highlighting the performance of gender through creating a trickster Virgin and a transvestite Caesar/Christ is undercut and diminished, however, by the novel's lack of sympathy for "the Little Virgin's" cold-blooded manipulation of gender roles, which it links to Ruth's obsession with parental betrayal. Letitia's Ulyssean reply, "I am no one," to Ruth's query, "Who are you?" (*Plague,* 12), in the novel's opening scene comes horribly true at her death, when her son steals her identity and her body is left unclaimed in the morgue. The punishments for emotionally abandoning a child are severely visited upon the parents in this novel, as in *The Last of the Crazy People*. Yet by suggesting that there might be some connection between Letitia and Race, the two "watchers" who accompany Ruth on her voyage home, the novel also suggests that "the Little Virgin" exists less as a person than as a concept, and that the virgin model of womanhood she embodies is as deadly and as attractive as the concept of "Race."

The novel is simply trying to do too much in too compressed and too confused a fashion. The germs of all of Findley's later work may be detected in embryo here. Ironically, his greatest innovation—the combination of a critique of the patriarchal family with a critique of the culmination of Western civilization in the Nazi holocaust—seems partly to blame for the critical neglect of this novel. When Findley separates these strands more decisively, addressing the Nazi theme in *Famous Last Words* and the family chronicle in *The Piano Man's Daughter,* the critical response is more positive.

The title, *The Butterfly Plague,* encapsulates the difficulty of this highly compressed and ambiguous novel. In its virtuoso display of mastery of a variety of narrative styles, the novel itself risks dismissal as a mere butterfly, a beautiful but inconsequential thing. Furthermore, conventional ways of thinking are challenged by a title that asks us to imagine butterflies, usually associated with beauty, fragility, and freedom, as the carriers of disaster, their very presence constituting a plague. The title may seem plausible as a way of describing Hollywood's increasing domination of film and television images, but it seems woefully inaccurate as a doubled metaphor for both Nazi atrocities and the sufferings they cause their victims. In the novel, the butterflies are both the cause of the plague and the chief victims of the plague.

According to Lorraine York, *The Butterfly Plague* describes a "search for Paradise in a fallen world" (York, *Front Lines,* 63). Such a quest connects Hollywood with the Nazis through a perfectionism and idealism that, taken to an extreme, can turn into a plague. Donna Palmateer Pennee elaborates on this description, arguing that "*The Butterfly Plague* demonstrates that like Hitler's Germany, Hollywood's dream factory sought to promulgate an ideal of physical beauty and to append nationalism to that physical ideal, to promote, propagandize, and legitimate all-American perfection" (Pennee, *Moral,* 29). *The Butterfly Plague,* then, suggests the dream turned nightmare, the ways in which idealized imaginings of human perfection can turn terribly wrong, transforming the quest for something better into a destructive evil. The butterfly plague, in these readings, stands for a morality that holds physical beauty as the highest good. Even the beautiful, such as butterflies, are victimized by such a belief.

This interpretation of the novel privileges the insights offered by Naomi in the mother-daughter conversation that forms the heart of the novel. In arguing that to be human is to be flawed, and that we must learn to accept these flaws as part of our nature, Naomi shows herself incapable of accepting her own daughter's "flaw"—a prophetic dreaming that challenges commonsense notions of reality. Naomi argues: "But the greatest flaw of all, the very worst, the most destructive and the seat of all our woes and pain, is this *dream*—this damnable quest for perfection" (*Plague*, 156). Her insight to this point seems fully endorsed by the rest of the novel, but she continues to assess the applicability of this theory to Ruth: "[W]hen I think of the misery and despair caused by people like you who will not accept—and who will not cope with reality as it is, I find it small wonder that humanity is condemned to suffering" (156). Ruth is othered in the phrase "people like you." Ruth protests: "But I do accept reality . . . It's only different from yours" (156). This dispute cannot be resolved as a simple matter of relative realities when one of Ruth's dreams involves the reality of the holocaust, an indisputable fact. Yet Ruth can only tell her story of the concentration camps indirectly, through creating a parallel narrative of the holocaust in Alvarez Canyon. The dream of Alvarez Canyon is a coded way of speaking the unspeakable. Her first impression of the camps as a kind of zoo creates a metaphorical crossing over to connect that experience with the nature preserve of the canyon. Her difficulty in communicating the reality of her vision, which turns on the associative patterns unleashed by a word or a sense perception, seems to replicate the novelist's challenge in learning to make his readers share his own distinctive way of representing the world.

In Naomi's view, Ruth's "dreams" represent a turning away from reality, an inability to accept her own imperfection, and a need to immerse herself in submission to a stronger force: to swimming, to Bruno, to Race. But Ruth and the narrator, while acknowledging that side of her character, also insist that she has something important to offer the world as a result of her experiences. Her vision of human suffering cannot be denied. Her accusation, *"They put out their hands to us,* Mother, and I was watching. But you turned away to watch something else" (153), accuses the world of inattention, not just to the horrors of the camps, a matter of historical documentation, but also to the suffering that happens around us and because of us every day. Ruth's love of swimming and her desire to perfect herself led her to the heart of Nazi Germany, a terrible outcome for her idealistic intentions. Naomi's decision to have children despite being a carrier of hemophilia led to the eventual breakup of her family and the disease of her son. Yet Ruth and Naomi agree that it would be worse to allow second guessing the impact of one's decisions to stop one from acting at all.

The Butterfly Plague suggests that engagement in the messy encounters that constitute life is preferable to withdrawal from it. Assuming that there is no safe place of retreat from the evils of the world, the novel consistently champions those characters who choose to risk attachments to others (such as Ruth and her mother, Naomi) over those who deny their affective links with others (such as Ruth's father, George, and Letitia Virden, the characters most dramatically associated with the urge to stop time and arrest change.) Characters such as Ruth's brother, Dolly, and Letitia's son, Octavius, who at first hide from the world and later decide to enter it, are commended for their decisions to move forward, even though such a decision leads to Dolly's death. Indeed, Dolly's bloody death is described as a sexual consummation in which he has finally met his dream, the beautiful androgynous child, Octavius, with "a face so young that it looked unborn. The sort of face the gods must have . . ." (306). When Dolly is dead, the narrator comments: "But wasn't it wonderful. The very last thing the dying man had heard had been his own name. On the lips of his dream" (320).

From the opening chapter the novel has enacted a series of deaths marking endings, clearing the way for the final chapter to make a fresh beginning. But the first version of the novel, through its inclusion of a final chronicle that has been omitted from the revised version, ties up loose ends and tries to impose a kind of closure through generational continuity by granting Ruth her wish to bear a child, a daughter who, it is implied, will carry on the family line and the family curse. Such an ending highlights the family chronicle over the story of the individual and the acceptance of human imperfections as the price of life, a double focus that anticipates the affirmative ending of The Piano Man's Daughter.

The change in the ending of the revised text constitutes the most dramatic difference between the two versions of the novel. Both are divided into Four Books containing a series of named chronicles whose titles, dates, and places are identical except for the final chronicle. In the first version, the book ends with "The Chronicle of Fire," which takes the story from 1939 to 1968, documenting the second marriage and early death of Ruth and depicting the meeting of her only surviving child, Lisa (whom the text inexplicably renames Lissl partway through the chronicle), with the son of Noah Telford, who had been a neighbor of the Damarosch family at Topanga Beach. Noah's son tells Lissl the story of the "Butterfly Plague" and witnesses with her the beginning of the Fire Plague. Commenting explicitly on how we are to read the paradoxes of the text, the narrator states: "We know that history repeats itself. We also know that it does not."[12]

In the revised version, the reader is left to infer this contradictory knowledge from "The Chronicle of the Exodus," which leaves Ruth in 1939 as the only survivor of her family, feeling "like Eve deserted in a whispering Eden. Unmanned" (*Plague*, 370), as the narrator oddly puts it, meditating on history and waiting for rain. Six feet tall and with very short hair, Ruth has always been an androgynous figure. The ending of the first version placed her firmly back within a heterosexual model of family reproduction that marked the end of her life as an individual. The revised version hints that the child to whom she wished to give birth was herself. Symbolically, her return to the predivorce family home at Falconridge is a return to the beginnings of the human story in a Garden of Eden preceding sexual divisions into male and female.

When the rain comes in a deluge and she has scattered the mingled ashes of her dead family, "[T]here was nothing to do but turn around and go" (374). These are the final words of the revised text. The earlier version had ended somewhat more ominously: "And thus, this Chronicle is over—the last of the Chronicles of the Butterfly Plague. The first of the Fire Plague. And . . ." (*Plague* 1969, 376). The first ending focused on the impersonal events of history. The revised ending focuses on Ruth. This revised ending aligns Ruth much more closely with Hooker and Iris at the end of *The Last of the Crazy People* and with Lucy and Mrs. Noyes at the end of *Not Wanted on the Voyage*. It is a rewriting that reinscribes Ruth as an innocent watcher who is learning to be a survivor. Ruth may have willed and dreamed the deaths of her immediate family, but unlike Hooker she pulled no triggers.

The revised version is more open-ended than the first version, leaving Ruth alive and embarking anew on the journey of her life despite the heavy baggage of sorrows and memories that she must bear. The first version overdetermines her victimhood through marking her as a triple victim: of genetics (she carries hemophilia), of history (she marries an abusive Nazi), and finally of fate (she dies in a car accident, as had her brother and father before her). In that ending, she lives on only through

her daughter. The revised version leaves her "[u]nmanned" (370), "like a
lone survivor" (371), feeling abandoned, "like a hostess whose most
popular guests have departed" (372), strangely emptied out of prior
identities and open to new hailings of the person she might become.
Academic theorists will be interested to note that in this description of
Ruth, Findley repeats the same image that the French philosopher Louis
Althusser employs to describe his famous notion of "interpellation," the
manner in which a person is "hailed" or called into a sense of identity by
the agents of the institutional state apparatuses employed to educate
and discipline: "Even her own vocation and her own fame had left her.
She felt no sense of place or position, felt as though someone—perhaps a
policeman—might challenge her presence the next time she walked or
wanted to walk down the street" (372). Such a state is vulnerable but
also open to new possibilities of identity formation.

The idyllic descriptions of nature, with flowers pressing against the
house, and insects and birds crowding thickly in anticipation of rain,
lead to the assertion that "[t]his was that sudden season of change—
constant in nature and in history" (373). Ruth spreads the mingled
ashes of her dead in this place that is alive with the possibility of
renewal, implying that the story of her doomed family (their house, Falconridge, nicknamed "Dunsinane" {370} in tribute to a hubris that
rivaled Macbeth's) may prove cathartic in the manner of a Shakespearean tragedy.

Whereas Hooker's internal violence erupted in the literal obliteration
of his family, Ruth's violence erupts and overflows from her dreams. She
is the sole witness of two murders and two fires, but it is impossible to
be sure if she has imagined them or actually caused them. Through such
ambiguities, the reader is made complicit in the madness of her visions.
Whereas Hooker and Cassandra are incarcerated for their madness,
Ruth is left free at the end of her story to begin again. She has witnessed
both her father's tyrannies and Nazi atrocities, internalized these horrors, and recycled them through her dreams. Everyone around her has
self-destructed. She has inherited the ruins of their dreams and the illusion of a freedom to begin again.

Chapter Three

"Broken Dreamers": Redefining Heroism

The Wars established Findley's fame as a major writer and *Famous Last Words* consolidated that position. Each novel uses the backdrop of war to question conventional definitions of ideal masculinity and the notion of the hero. In *The Wars,* Robert Ross is remembered for a puzzling act that some condemn and others praise as the ultimate in heroism. His act, although it incurs a terrible martyrdom, inspires a retrospective search for understanding that composes the substance of the book. *Famous Last Words* provides an idiosyncratic view of the Second World War from the point of view of Hugh Selwyn Mauberley, an American aesthete and fascist sympathizer, and thus an unlikely hero, who is murdered in the Alps by a Nazi hit man just before the end of the war. Mauberley's heroism, if such it can be called, consists in his compulsive witnessing to the atrocities of his times. Although the bodies of both men are horribly broken, their testaments, in the shape of the lives they lived and the impact they have on others, survive. I have borrowed the phrase, "broken dreamers" (*Headhunter,* 271) from Marlow's thoughts on the human race in Findley's *Headhunter* because it so aptly captures the doubleness and ambiguities of these men's fates.

In *The Wars,* Robert's story is pieced together by a researcher arranging fragments from archives and imaginatively seeking entry to a closed past. Much of Mauberley's story in *Famous Last Words* is told in the first person by Mauberley himself, written with a silver pencil on the walls of the Grand Elysium Hotel before his pursuer caught up to him and tried to silence his story by murdering him. Findley's radio play, *The Trials of Ezra Pound,* continues the investigation into the modernist notion of the artist as hero and its connection to the betrayal, rather than the fulfillment, of conventional expectation. Findley believes that "[a]rt must menace. Sure, it can be gentle menace but it must make you feel uncomfortable. Beauty should make you feel uncomfortable."[1] These three problematic Findley heroes embody the menace and discomfort of beauty in the images and words they leave behind.

Out of the Archives

In *The Last of the Crazy People* and *The Butterfly Plague,* what Hooker and Ruth, as innocent watchers, actually "see" cannot be told directly. Their intuitive perceptions can only be approximated through implication, double entendres, puns, and doublings of various kinds, and through patterns of imagery that seemed impenetrably ambiguous to many readers at the time the novels first were published. In *Crazy People* and *The Butterfly Plague,* the central characters' perceptions can seldom clearly be distinguished from those of the omniscient narrators'. Both narrators and characters seem equally bewildered by the dilemma described in *The Wars* as "what cannot be told."[2] In *The Wars,* however, a clearer distinction is drawn between what the central character, Robert Ross, cannot articulate and what the text itself, through its various narrators, cannot say. The narrative position of the researcher in *The Wars* provides a preliminary point of reference for the reader that establishes Robert as a shared figure of desire for researcher and reader alike. Because Robert, unlike Hooker and Ruth, is characterized as almost inarticulate, a man who prefers action above words, he provides a silent center for the interpretative quest that constitutes the act of reading. And because he has been dead for many years when the novel opens with the researcher's quest, the mystery his motivations present remains plausibly explicable as the inaccessibility of history itself.

Readers responded enthusiastically to *The Wars* as a novel that was as much about the search to understand the past as it was about a young Canadian soldier's experiences in the First World War. The double narrative of the novel records two stories: the researcher's attempt to reconstruct Robert's story from the fragmented evidence that has survived from the past, and an anonymous narrator's presentation of scenes from Robert's life that are logically unavailable to the researcher but that are intuitively available for reconstruction to the novelizing imagination. Some interpretations privilege the first story; others, the second. Critics who focus on Robert's story tend to describe the book as modernist; critics who focus on the problems of interpretation posed by the text describe it as postmodernist. In this chapter I examine how the interdependence of the two stories is central to the experience of reading and understanding this book, and argue that the text's negotiations between modernist and postmodernist impulses mark it as essentially postcolonial. In using postcolonial in this context, I am suggesting primarily the need to decolonize the imagination from the inherited assumptions of

Eurocentric systems that encompass both the modernist and the post-modernist understandings of art and the forms of knowledge it conveys. Postmodernism is suspicious of all grand narratives, but Findley wishes to hold on to a grand narrative of human community and continuity that transcends the localized scope of the Westernized imagination. A writer cannot decolonize the imagination by a simple act of will but he can suggest the need for shifts in thinking that might begin to enable such a revolution. Findley begins that process in *The Wars*.

With the benefit of hindsight, one can find new meanings in Findley's early novels through the avenues of perception opened up by the later ones. *The Wars* marks the turning point in the consolidation of Findley's vision. The tyranny of families, the horrors of civilization, and the redemption offered by the natural world here fuse into a celebration of endurance offered, like Rodwell's last words to his daughter (themselves an echo of Prospero's final words in Shakespeare's *The Tempest*), as "prayers against despair" (*Wars*, 135). *The Wars* is his most perfectly realized novel, emotionally cathartic, aesthetically satisfying, and intellectually troubling. Its insistence on the fundamental undecidedness of judgment enables readers to read their own uncertainties and certainties into its story of a young man who does not want to grow up on the terms dictated to him by his society. For some critics, however, the ambiguities of this novel affirm the very values the text seems designed to question.

In "Homoerotic Capitalism: *The Wars*," Frank Davey sees that through its silences, the novel "risks being recuperated as an ingenious narrative (Vauthier), or as a critique merely of war (Thompson)."[3] Indeed, early criticism of *The Wars* focuses most attention on its complex narrative technique, on its relation to the genre of war literature, or on its thematic message in relation to war. Almost all this early criticism is appreciative and explanatory in nature. Davey dissents strongly from the consensus that has established *The Wars* as canonically central to the Canadian literary tradition. Against celebrations of the novel's narrative complexity and liberal humanist vision, Davey (following earlier suggestions made by Dennis Duffy) argues that *The Wars* irresponsibly "constructs all authority as male, homoerotic, and savage" (Davey, 121) and that the only alternative to "homoerotic phallic authority . . . is a relationship to an animal" (122). This is a provocatively reductive reading that fails to do justice to Findley's use of animals in his fiction, but it points to certain problems in the novel's vision that do require addressing. "There is," Davey argues, "an enormous silence in the novel about

what a culture might do once it had moved from the violently phallic
norms presented here" (125). Davey's argument itself risks dismissal for
its conflation of phallic authority with the penis, and its conflation of the
homoerotic, homosexual, and homosocial, and has been critiqued on
these grounds by Heather Sanderson and Tom Hastings.[4] Nonetheless,
his argument is a useful reminder that this novel is very much a product
of its time and place: nationalist Canada in a mood of postcentenary celebrations (which had culminated in Expo 67 in Montreal) during the
times of the Vietnam war protests and the beginnings of a renewed ecological movement, when many assumed the truth of the sixties slogans
"never trust anyone over thirty" and "give peace a chance." Such assumptions no longer seem self-evident. That does not mean that *The Wars* can
no longer speak to contemporary public debates, but that it necessarily
speaks to them differently.

Although Ruth tells "The Chronicle of the Nightmare" in the first
person, the rest of *The Butterfly Plague* emerges through the interplay
of an omniscient third-person narration with interventions from an
unknown first-person narrator who addresses the reader directly. *The
Last of the Crazy People* is told exclusively through an omniscient third-
person narrator. Narration in *The Wars* is much more complex, distributed among a number of voices. Simone Vauthier, in the most thorough
examination of this dimension of the novel, distinguishes between the
"nameless I-narrator" who is "essentially a mediator"; "his alter-ego"
(although gender is never specified); the anonymous researcher in the
archives who is addressed in the second person as "You" (and who may
or may not be the same person as the "I-narrator"); and a "third person
or impersonal narrator."[5] Transcriptions of taped episodes of first-person
testimony from two witnesses, Lady Juliet D'Orsey and Marian Turner,
also contribute to the narration. The "scriptor" arranges these fragments
of the novel's two stories (Robert's ordeal and the researcher's investigation into that past) in a way that throws into question the I-narrator's
claims to historicity. Although many critics refer to the researcher as the
archivist, it is clear that they are not the same person. The archivist is
identified as the woman in charge of the archives where the researcher is
examining the material left from Robert's life. By closing the archive as
night falls, she provides the novel with its final arbitrary yet appropriately consoling visual image as the researcher reaches out for one final
photograph to encapsulate the mood of the book.

This photograph, of Robert, his sister Rowena, and their pony, Meg,
with its caption reading "Look! You can see our breath!" (*Wars,* 191),

seems to confirm the epigraph from Euripedes that prefaces the novel: "Never that which is shall die." The final words of the novel, "And you can" (191), links past and present in a shared affirmation of the pricelessness of life as symbolized through breath. This is the equivalent of the markings on the cave at Altamira in *Famous Last Words,* a statement to the reader that these people and this pony were alive once and that their lives mattered. The effect of the whole chorus of narrative voices, in Vauthier's view, is to decenter the narrative and draw the reader more deeply into the collaborative act of making meaning, so that the act of reading becomes a rewriting and finally a shared "seeing" into the deeper significance of apparently innocuous photographs such as this one. Such a focus on making the reader see defines the modernist experiments of Joseph Conrad and Henry James, two writers whose names are mentioned in the story.

Robert's maimed and silent body becomes a cipher over which these various narrators write their readings of what Robert Ross means. It is this metafictional element of the novel, its awareness of itself as fiction, that has led to its classification by some critics as postmodernist. *The Wars* is obsessively concerned with how human beings make meaning through the shaping conventions of language and visual perception, and with those dimensions of experience that ruling representational conventions seem incapable of controlling.

The novel's framing opening scene of the horse on the railroad tracks (repeated near the end of the book) introduces this interest through its fascination with what "could not be told." Eve Kosofsky Sedgwick explains that the trope of the "unspeakable," a standard Gothic element, had a double literary function in the nineteenth-century English novel, referring to a Faustian pact and to a form of sexuality that after the trials of Oscar Wilde became more publicly accessible as "the Love that dare not speak its name."[6] With Oscar Wilde, in Sedgwick's analysis, "homosexual style—and homophobic style—instead of being stratified and specified and kept secret along lines of class, became . . . a household word—the word 'Oscar Wilde' " (Sedgwick, 216–17). By naming Robert Ross for Wilde's Canadian lover and literary executor, Findley invokes this intertext in *The Wars.* Juliet's two favorite books, Wilde's *The Picture of Dorian Gray* and Henry James's *The Turn of the Screw,* reinforce the novel's fascination with modernist inscriptions of ambiguity and their connection to the unspeakable.

The trope of the unspeakable also drives Conrad's *Heart of Darkness,* another modernist text that Findley rewrites most thoroughly in *Head-*

hunter. In *Heart of Darkness,* the unspeakable hints at cannibalism. In *The Wars,* the unspeakable is symbolized through the act of male rape, which Findley sees as metaphorically a type of cannibalism, in which the more powerful symbolically devour the weak. Robert's rape at the hands of his fellow officers in the baths of the asylum at Desolé is the novel's heart of darkness, marking the nadir of Robert's descent into hell. Robert discovers the irrational heart of European rationality and the violence that underpins European civilization not in the wilderness and not at the hands of the mad but within the social structures designed to contain and discipline such forces and at the hands of those with the authority to run them: in the asylum for the insane and the military. Unlike Conrad's Kurtz, Robert does not surrender to these forces, although he recognizes stirrings within himself that are capable of such a response. Instead, he burns his sister's portrait, as "an act of charity" the text reports (172), perhaps to protect the symbol of her innocence from the horror of such knowledge, and then he proceeds to act, as she would have, out of compassion for the weak when the opportunity first arises. Given a choice between obedience to the rapacity of the officers in charge of the war and the forming of an alliance with the animals who still cling to life, Robert chooses the animals. That act reverses normal social hierarchies of value, therefore marking him as insane or deviant from the point of view of the authorities he has rejected.

The plural title of the novel has led most critics to assume that it refers to more than military conflicts, but there is some disagreement about how "the wars" signifies. In " 'A Shout of Recognition': 'Likeness' and the Art of Simile in Timothy Findley's *The Wars,*" Lorraine York argues that Findley recasts the "inconceivable" realities of war in the "guise of the familiar," tying this foreign condition to a stable, familiar state of being."[7] In other words, domestic conflicts are used to explain military conflict to a largely civilian readership. For York, Findley's primary interest is in war itself and how it has shaped our century. I see war as an unstable metaphor (rather than a simile) attuning the reader to how violence functions within civil and military contexts. Most readers are familiar with the conventions of the war novel, war movie, and war televison show. War, as a representational concept, is as familiar to the twentieth-century audience as peace. The parallels between domestic and military violence in *The Wars* are not necessary to make war understandable; instead, they work to defamiliarize the familiar, showing that the world readers are accustomed to accepting as normal (and opposing to war) is in actuality itself constructed by violently unequal conditions of oppression. Class wars, gender wars, and colonial wars all constitute the world of peacetime Canada and Britain in Findley's *The Wars*. In other words, the military war is less the focus of interest in this novel and more the vehicle for revealing the violent conditions of everyday life that readers have learned to accept as normal. Conventional notions of the military are also problematized, however, as are ideas about what constitutes heroic behavior. *The Wars,* like all of Findley's work, argues the truth of Walter Benjamin's maxim that "[t]here is no document of civilization which is not at the same time a document of barbarism."[8] War and peace are equally implicated in this understanding.

To make this argument is not to deny the validity of Evelyn Cobley's claim that *"The Wars* is marked by a self-conscious reworking of the war genre which situates it clearly in a postmodern and post-Vietnam world."[9] Cobley believes that "the war context has been too easily ignored" through readings that place the novel "in the context of Canadian literature or postmodern metafiction" (Cobley, 98). Each of these contexts is important for understanding the novel, but I would argue that these different contexts are connected through Findley's interrogation of Western civilization as a whole and its promotion of aggression and a narrow utilitarianism as the models for male behavior.

The Wars' focus on the disguised continuities (and not on the discontinuity) between war and everyday life links concerns about the status of knowledge and how we know what we know with concerns about imperialism, gender relations, and other forms of naturalized violence. Findley parallels the Signals Office and the Stock Exchange (*Wars,* 115), the emotions of the high school football game and war (165), the mindlessness of the factory conveyer belt and the rhythms of war (175), the unthinking disciplines of school and the military (29), and the mechanical prostitution of the whorehouse and the crazy dance of war (40). These comparisons encourage drawing connections between apparent opposites, but they also require readers to interrogate the habit of mind that too quickly tries to see a connecting pattern in everything.

There are two terrors determining the novel's complex form of narration: a terror of meaninglessness and a terror of meanings too easily made, of conclusions drawn from unexamined assumptions. These twin terrors are both connected to forms of silence, or what cannot be told. For example, polite society does not speak of its foundations on brutality. Canada's foundations on conquest—of the Indians and then of the French—can be told only indirectly, through reference to Robert's first hero, the native runner Tom Longboat (a real historical personage and not an invention), whom he makes into a mythic avatar of freedom; to the Indians he sees standing at the side of the track as his train rushes by, who are characterized as "ghosts through the frosted glass" (69), silent reminders of past wrongs; and to the Indians who, legend has it, have cut out the big Swede's tongue in times past, making his muteness a silent reminder of past wars on North American soil. Wolfe's conquest of Quebec is put in an imperial context by Robert's lover, the British-born Barbara D'Orsey (Juliet's older sister), but reclaimed for a nationalist one by Robert.

Silence is also a polite convention for maintaining social control. No one mentions Robert's mother's drinking (24), ostensibly to protect the family, yet in actuality this silence constitutes a refusal to acknowledge or to deal with her pain. Robert's mind stammers when he is faced with behavior or information that does not make sense within the expectations he has been taught. (Juliet experiences the same affliction.) Robert cannot speak of why he cannot satisfy the prostitute in Wet Goods nor of what he sees through the hole in the wall (his hero Taffler engaged in sadomasochistic sex with the big Swede), nor of his rape at the asylum. These are experiences that cannot be told in his culture because they challenge dominant assumptions about normal heterosexual male behavior (men are not supposed to have trouble performing sex with women; people are not supposed to take pleasure in giving or receiving pain; men are not supposed to have sex with other men, forced or consensual).

Rowena, Robert's hydrocephalic sister, represents another area of institutionalized silence. She is excluded from official family photographs because her infirmity challenges the norm of the ideal family. Robert loves Rowena and insists on placing her photograph on his bureau in defiance of the family's wish to keep her secret. The novel is silent about the nature of Robert's intense love for his sister, but the possibility of incest seems another taboo that is both invoked and buried. (In the movie version, he innocently asks her to marry him.)

Through its list of silenced characters and its fragmented narration, *The Wars* argues that conventional history can no longer be told. The historian's objectivity, like the researcher's, is a myth. Any telling necessarily silences alternative versions. Robert is characterized as a hero by some and a coward or a villain by others. Although the novel seeks to discredit the official view of Robert's disobedience and killing of two fellow officers as too narrowly defined, his rebellious gesture of killing people to save animals remains ambiguous. The narrator compares Robert to a series of explorers (Scott, Lawrence, Mallory) and one philosopher

(Euripides) who are linked through the shared fate of dying "obscured by violence" (11). Like them, it is implied, Robert has ventured into unknown territory, becoming himself an area of taboo. According to Marian Turner, Robert's nurse, "Robert did the thing that no one else would even dare to think of doing" (16). He questioned, not only the logic of war but of civilization itself.

To the army, Robert's behavior can be dismissed as disobedient and possibly insane, but none of the book's narrators find this explanation satisfactory. In an apparent questioning of the novel's second epigraph from von Clausewitz, the narrator privileges Robert's intent in trying to save the horses over the facts of disobedience, desertion, theft, and murder that are recorded in the transcript of the court martial. In the narrator's retelling, it is Captain Leather's orders that are mad, and Captain Leather's behavior that is reprehensible. The narrative implies that Ross was justified in shooting Captain Leather because his orders were both foolish and cruel, because he shot Robert's good friend Devlin, and because he threatened to shoot Robert. But if this were all Robert had done, he would not have inspired the complex emotions the researcher encounters as he tries to reconstruct what happened.

Robert's innovation was to speak of himself and the animals as a collective "we," recognizing his affinities with them as living creatures and denying the hierarchy that orders animal/human relations in the world at large as well as within the military. Earlier scenes of Robert's refusal to kill Rowena's rabbits, his sending postcards from the front to the family pets, his running with the coyote and later the horses, Harris's stories of swimming with the whales, and Rodwell's sketches of animals (which include Robert as the only human portrait), presage this final decision of Robert's to align himself with the horses and the dog against his fellow soldiers. Robert is internally violent (witness his attack on the tree) but he is not a killer. His angry cry, "What are soldiers for?" (25), when he sees his sister's soldier boyfriend standing by as the hired man kills Rowena's rabbits suggests that he thinks that a soldier's job is to protect lives and prevent killing. This is a view of the military promoted during the terms of office served by Prime Minister Lester Pearson (winner of the Nobel Peace Prize) and his successor, Pierre Elliott Trudeau. But Robert does not anthropomorphize animals. His mother wants to kill Rowena's rabbits because Rowena was playing with them when she fell from her chair to her death, but Robert does not blame the rabbits. He accepts them, like all animals, for what they are: different, and with an equal right to survive with dignity.

His gesture in trying to save the horses (and the rabbits before them) is fundamentally one of compassion, a dangerous emotion to indulge in times of war. (Compassion constitutes Amy Wylie's madness in *Headhunter* as well.) Robert knows this. When the German soldier spares his life in the crater, Robert's moment of distrust in the German's compassion leads him to kill his benefactor. Robert mistakes the German's binoculars for a gun. Robert's own gesture in freeing the horses is also misinterpreted, yet he chooses to align himself with life against death, and with uncertainties against certainty. Near the end of the book, the narrator quotes Nicholas Fagan, Findley's fictional alter ego: "*Nothing so completely verifies our perception of a thing as our killing of it*" (191). In *Crazy People,* Gilbert drunkenly killed Hooker's cat to "prove" that he had seen a red fox. By deferring meaning and affirming the mystery of Robert's life, the narrator refuses to "kill" Robert Ross again by privileging one perception of Robert against those advanced by the other voices in the text. He chooses the "shout of recognition" (191) over the "shot" that kills. Therefore the novel develops a fictional language of patterns of repetition and substitution, what Cobley calls "echo scenes" (Cobley, 114), less to tell "what could not be told" than to defer meaning indefinitely. Robert's brutally maimed and burnt body, the mystery of his unusual gesture of aligning himself with the animals, and his refusal of an easy death remain to haunt the reader. His body is broken but his spirit is not.

Juliet describes Robert as a "true athlete" who seeks "beauty through perfection" (*Wars,* 103), linking the athlete's quest to the artist's, as a way of expressing the love she saw between Robert and Harris, the invalid storyteller. Robert finds a hero and mentor in Taffler, another athlete, and a confidante in Harris. Robert also finds a community of other men who worship beauty in the stained glass dugout. Each of these friends, like Robert, is a dreamer who is broken by the violence of the war, Rodwell perhaps most horribly. Yet it is Rodwell who writes the life-affirming letter to his daughter, entrusted to Robert, promising that "[w]e survive in one another" (135). This communal vision implicitly questions the individualism that defines the traditional war hero.

Marian Turner articulates the novel's aesthetic of the broken dreamer: "I guess you saw them all as beautiful because you couldn't bear to see them broken" (16). The civilized atmosphere of the dugout has been created through the salvaging of broken fragments of Christian art. The dugout is a microcosm of the novel as a whole: a place where fragments of memories console shell-shocked survivors for the violent destruction of their worlds. Devlin collects old glass, Rodwell small animals in his makeshift hospital, and Levitt quotations from books, just as the researcher collects photographs, letters, newspaper clippings, and tapes—to reconstruct a lost time and place, life beyond the reach of the war. In a phrase that can be taken to define the novel's aesthetic, Devlin introduces himself as a man "devoted to fragility" (87). His stained glass door is beautiful rather than functional: it does not close. It depicts St. Eloi working at a forge holding aloft a grotesque butterfly just recovered from the flames. This echo of *The Butterfly Plague* need not be identified for the reader to see the symbolism of the butterfly as the beauty of fragility and the fire as both a destructive and a creative force. Like St. Eloi's butterfly, Robert emerges from his own personal holocaust of fire, a grotesque yet strangely beautiful new creature.

The banquet celebrated in the stained glass dugout with the food Robert has brought echoes Plato's *Symposium* with the philosophical all-male conversation a camp parody of overrefined sensibilities that makes it seem very European to North American ears. Rodwell's Toad is promoted to the rank of Field Marshall, and moody Bonnycastle (in an echo of T. S. Eliot's Prufrock) rhapsodizes, "I do like a peach," and then mourns that "[t]he peaches have made me sad" (91). Here is a moral touchstone to oppose to the madness of Captain Leather, whose name associates him with male violence in Findley's thematic lexicon. (Dangerous men always trail scents of leather, from Letitia's attendants in *The Butterfly Plague* to Mauberley's assassin in *Famous Last Words*.) These men in the dugout enact alternative models for masculinity. Even the humorless Levitt, who seems the spoilsport in the group, has brought books in his bag to the front rather than the supplies more usually associated with the job of the soldier. It is true that each of these men dies a horrible death, yet each must be judged for how he lived his life. As Juliet says: "The thing is . . . to clarify who you are through your response to when you lived" (103). The clarifications they provide live for the reader in the text.

It is also true that the dugout haven provides no role for women. Women in this novel play many other roles, but they are not associated with the beauty of fragility. They function as resistant witnesses to the dominant view of Robert as murderer and coward, like Juliet and Marian; as symbols of lost innocence, like Rowena; as monstrously phallic, like Barbara; or as a secret sharer in Robert's torment, like his mother, Mrs. Ross, who vicariously suffers everything he experiences except for his hope for the future, embodied in the enigmatic words he speaks to Marian when offered a premature death, "Not yet." Women are excluded from the dugout embodiment of the fragility/beauty equation in this novel because they have conventionally monopolized this role in pioneer societies such as Canada. Findley's novel seeks to reclaim this aesthetic for men as well.

Robert justifies his release of the horses by saying that they will be needed, but his attraction to them springs from their beauty. They are beautiful to him because they are wholly alive in a world dedicated to its own destruction, and they remind him of his own physicality and his love of running. The horse suggests the physical perfection Robert seeks as an athlete, the masculine sexuality he fears in himself, and, in the form of Pegasus, the ability of the imagination to soar above the limitations of reality. For a Canadian reader, the novel's opening image of the horse on the train tracks invokes Canadian Alex Colville's canonical painting "Horse and Train" (1954), with its dramatic visual image of the unevenly weighted confrontation between a technology dependent on the animal body and a technology of the machine. The horse, symbol of a way of life that is under threat from the machine, is a doomed creature whose inevitable passing is mourned in this image. Robert also, as a compassionate man trying to hold on to his humanity in the theater of war, is presented as a type of endangered species.

The Wars argues that beauty is most visible and most vulnerable when it is under threat, as in times of war or in a society that devalues it. The novel locates beauty in four central areas: in childhood, in nature, in male friendship, and in those society would see as physically damaged. Each category of the beautiful is distinguished by fragility and marked as transitory. Robert's devotion to these fragile beauties makes it difficult for him to grow up into the manhood his society prescribes for him. He is a Canadian Huck Finn, seeking the lost past of his childhood but incapable of lighting out for new territory. Robert's parents are reading *Huckleberry Finn* on their way to say good-bye to him as he leaves for the war. The narrator ends his account of their farewell with a quotation from Twain's novel: "*Come on back to the raf', Huck honey*" (70). Mrs. Ross is watching her husband and son say farewell, thinking of the accidental early death of her beloved brother, from which she has never recovered. It is unclear whether this quotation is meant to be her thought, her characterization of her husband and son's farewell, or the narrator's summation, but the effect is one of campy disorientation. Jim's black dialect and the homoerotic associations of his idyll on the raft with Huck is appropriated as the language and imagery through which this uptight, Anglo-Saxon Canadian family expresses its desire to remain intact in its protected world of childhood innocence, oblivious of racial or military hatreds.

Findley's imagery returns Robert to a version of this peace in his final years as an invalid in the care of Juliet, but first he must experience its demonic opposite in the dike scene where the sound of lapping waters reminds him of the raft at Jackson's Point, his childhood cottage (and a resort for the wealthy elite in this period). On the battlefield, however, the sound is not the unspoiled natural world but a nature polluted by the floating corpses of the war dead. Instead of problematizing Robert's idyllic image of childhood innocence at Jackson's Point, the novel seems to endorse it as a touchstone of Wordsworthian communion with nature before it is destroyed by the darkening years of growing up that culminate in the horror of war. Robert's lost innocence as an individual becomes the lost innocence of the political order destroyed by the First World War and the lost innocence of his country, Canada, forced to participate in a European war. This romanticization of an earlier period of aristocratic privilege, childhood innocence, and communion with nature characterizes the canon of English literature as celebrated by F. R. Leavis. Findley's ambivalence about this heritage erupts in the text at moments such as this.

For Robert, as for Ruth in *The Butterfly Plague,* the journey to Europe is not a voyage into that idealized past but rather into the heart of darkness. Findley reverses Conrad's classic narrative of the European regression into the African heart of darkness to record North American journeys into the supposed heart of Western civilization only to discover there the brutality that Europeans projected outwards onto the countries they colonized. Although broken by her dreams, Ruth returns to the dream of a new beginning at the end of *The Butterfly Plague.* For Robert Ross, there is no fresh beginning, but his ordeal by fire implies the renewal that comes with the myth of the phoenix.

Reading the Walls

The epigraph to *Famous Last Words* is taken from a historical novel dealing with imperial Rome by Findley's mentor, Thornton Wilder: " . . . one does not know what one knows, or even what one wishes to know, until one is challenged and must lay down a stake."[10] The epigraph from Wilder implies a connection between the decline and fall of the Roman Empire and that of the European empires that flourished at the end of the nineteenth century and were decolonized throughout the twentieth century. The epigraph also suggests that the fascination with the process of making knowledge and constructing values that drove the story of

The Wars will be taken up again in *Famous Last Words,* where they are addressed through the late change of heart experienced by the novel's chief protagonist, Hugh Selwyn Mauberley, as he witnesses and records the terrible repercussions of his flirtation with fascism. By writing his story on the walls of the hotel where he meets his death, Mauberley lays down his stake. But has he laid it down on the side of truth or lies? And how can the reader decide? This is the puzzle that continues to fascinate and frustrate readers of this enigmatic novel. The double structure of the novel anticipates reader response and attempts to direct it by alternating between Mauberley's story as he has written it on the walls and the violently different responses to Mauberley's narrative of the American soldiers who discover and read it after his death.

Although Findley did not come up with the idea of using the character of Hugh Selwyn Mauberley to focus this story until he was into his fifth draft, Mauberley seems, in retrospect, an ideal and inevitable choice. Findley took Mauberley's name and character from Ezra Pound's canonical modernist poem *Hugh Selwyn Mauberley.* He is a fictional character, invented and satirized by Pound, who is retrieved and rehabilitated by Findley. Findley gives this rather one-dimensional persona from Pound's poem a fully fleshed out life and context and the opportunity to provide a fuller apologia for his life. Findley's novel thus enters into dialogue with Pound on the vexed question of the artist's responsibilities to his world.

Pound's poem dramatizes "a conflict between the antithetical demands of aestheticism and politics," recording the tragedy of "the *pure* aesthete."[11] Pound's ironic poem functions as "a series of intertextual parodies."[12] Findley's novel extends the parodic play to question Pound's aesthetic and its influence. Critics disagree about how to read Findley's reinscription of Pound's poem (in fragments as epigraphs to various chapters, in imagery, and in verbal echoes), and in the characterization of Mauberley. David Williams argues that the parody leads the reader to question Mauberley's integrity. Linda Hutcheon and Stephen Scobie believe that the parody endorses Mauberley's aesthetic. Scobie concludes a lengthy analysis of this dimension of the novel with the conclusion that Findley's Mauberley is distinguished by the "heroism of his bearing witness."[13] Linda Hutcheon concurs, arguing that the novel comments through Mauberley on "the silence of aestheticism."[14] David Williams, in contrast, believes that Mauberley embodies the worst sins of aestheticism, concluding that Mauberley's "ultimate decadence is to imply the greater truth of masks than of men."[15] For Williams, *"Famous Last Words* reifies the 'triumph' of beauty over truth by letting the aesthete speak"

(Williams, 260). While Williams is surely correct in identifying the influence of Oscar Wilde on the construction of Mauberley's aestheticism, his denunciation of the novel pays insufficient attention, in my view, to the novel's enactment of a debate between the advocate of truth as beauty (as represented by the soldier Quinn's reading of Mauberley's text on the wall) and the advocate of truth as a power relation (as represented by the soldier Freyberg's reading). The novel is not so fully under the sway of a pure aestheticism as Williams insists, although it does finally advocate seeing the writer as a kind of hero for telling the world unpalatable truths about itself.

Mauberley is a writer whose life and words become inseparable, and who pays with his life for that relation. But first of all he is a son. The preface of the novel, dated 1910, establishes Mauberley as the innocent product of the typical Findley family, with an inconsolably unhappy mother and a bewildered father who does not know how to make her happy. His father leaps to his death, leaving his son the silver pencil and a model for evading life through abdication. (In *Headhunter,* Warren Ellis's father will dance to his death in the presence of his son, leaping out of a window high up in a boardroom. Such dramatic scenes of a father abandoning his son often mark the heritage that the Findley hero must negotiate.) Much later, Quinn reveals that Mauberley's mother "had lost her mind because she was obsessed with perfection she could not achieve as a pianist" (*Words,* 155–56). This embedded family narrative implies that Mauberley has inherited his need to embrace the dream of perfection through fascism, first embodied for him in the mask of the powerful woman who would be queen, Wallis Simpson, who instead became the Duchess of Windsor when the King of England abdicated his throne to marry her.

The parallel story of the duke and duchess comments further on the nature of heroism. As heir to the throne, and briefly king, the duke was a charismatic icon of power and charm to millions. When he abdicated his throne, he became, with his wife, an icon of another kind: one of the power of love to conquer other dreams. The abdication recurs in Findley's narratives as one of those determinant public demarcations of memory after which nothing can ever be the same again. Findley's story shows the man behind the mask, and the woman behind the man, revealing the emptiness behind the icons. When the duke confronts himself in his hall of mirrors, he sees nothing but his failure to live up to the power of the icon. Writing this story on the walls of his hotel, Mauberley records the failures of the duke to provide the leadership demanded by his role, first as king and later as duke. In contrast, Isabella Loverso demonstrates the integrity and decisiveness of a true hero, providing an inspiration to Mauberley to change his allegiances.

In March 1945, as the war draws to a close, Mauberley abandons Rapallo and his surrogate father, the poet Ezra Pound, seeking asylum in the hotel high in the mountains where he produces his testament and meets his death. This introduction of real historical people, such as Ezra Pound and the Duke and Duchess of Windsor, into a fictional account of historical events reminds the reader that *Famous Last Words* is a historical novel. Usually real historical personages play minor roles in historical fiction, enabling the author to create an aura of authenticity without being tied too narrowly to the facts. In *Famous Last Words,* Findley stretches this convention, inventing public commitments and private scenes for the Duke and Duchess of Windsor that have long been matters of speculation but that have never been fully documented, and professing to offer a solution to a murder (that of Sir Harry Oakes) that has never in fact been solved. Every critic writing on this novel has discussed its status as a kind of historical fiction that blurs the distinctions between fact and fiction to convey its author's notion of truth. Thus the style of Findley's omniscient narrator mirrors that of Mauberley himself, occasionally blurring the boundaries between the two, so it is not always clear who is responsible for which text. Although Williams finds this technique irresponsible, other critics praise it for highlighting the difficulties of writing and reading in a postmodern age.

Mauberley is being stalked by enemies who wish to kill not only him but "his words as well" (21). What he writes is feared for the evidence it provides of the guilt and complicities of the powerful. His notebooks are described in a haunting metaphor as being "feared like a morgue where the dead are kept on ice—with all their incriminating wounds intact" (21). The metaphor of the morgue becomes literal in chapter two, in which the American soldier Annie Oakley is described as "the Keeper of the Morgue" because he guards the corpses piled in the saloon of the Grand Elysium Hotel after Mauberley's body has been found (57). This metaphor (in which notebooks, hotel, and novel each become a kind of morgue) attests to the human cost of war. Although war deaths are not usually classified as murders, Findley's language suggests that they should be. Mauberley's words and Findley's novel act as "incriminating wounds." They accuse.

As in *The Butterfly Plague,* Findley's horror is directed as much at the people who pleaded ignorance as it is at those who perpetuated the crimes of war. Mauberley's narrative invalidates the excuses of those in power who deny knowing what the Nazis were up to. Mauberley's refusal to accept his friends' alibis makes him unpopular with everyone. Before Mauberley leaves Rapallo, Ezra Pound's Italian home, Pound complains that he has made himself an "arse-eyed traitor to the whole world!" (7). As with Robert Ross, the reader must decide if Mauberley is a traitor or a hero for his insistence on recording what he has seen.

Findley has described the writer as a combination of voyeur, eavesdropper, and tour guide out of hell who accompanies his characters "into the void—and help[s] them find their way home" ("Alice," 12, 16). Mauberley's record takes on all these functions, recording the intimate details of the lives of the rich and famous: the rise and fall of the Penelope Cabal, a group dedicated to the fascist reinstallation of the Duke of Windsor as the Nazi-directed puppet King of England; the murder of the millionaire industrialist Sir Harry Oakes; and the engineered deaths of fascist sympathizers who defected when they realized the enormity of what was happening, and of others who merely got in the fascists' way, or were used and then discarded.

Like *The Butterfly Plague*'s "Chronicle of Alvarez Canyon," Mauberley's account of "The Spitfire Bazaar" displaces the holocaust from Europe to the Americas (this time to Bermuda). Instead of animals, the victims are the elite of colonial society and a hack journalist whose nickname echoes one of Dickens's most angelic heroines, Little Nell. It seems an odd form of substitution for addressing the holocaust, but it forces the reader to think beyond knee-jerk reactions to get to the heart of what is most horrifying in this historical legacy.

Mauberley's narrative locates enduring value in the imprint of a hand on the caves at Altamira. This record of primitive humans leads Mauberley to conclude, "I knew I was sitting at the heart of the human race—which is its will to say *I am*" (*Words,* 173). Significantly, Mauberley experiences this moment with Isabella Loverso, who herself embodies a belief in "the value of the human mind" and a willingness to hold words "against the sword" (42). Mauberley writes his narrative on the walls of her room at the hotel instead of his own. This location suggests that he is aligning his movement away from pure aestheticism toward a telling of the truth, and it is what enables his words to escape the detection of his killer, Harry Reinhardt.

Mauberley's words are received very differently by the two American soldiers who discover and read them. Freyberg is the resistant reader, suspicious of everything, while Quinn is the empathetic reader who suspends his own judgment to immerse himself in the world of the text. Both men care about justice, but Freyberg believes it should be enforced through legal systems of retribution and Quinn, fearing that such an approach could reinstall the very injustice it seeks to combat, believes that to do justice to the challenge of the Nazi camps will require an empathetic effort to understand how people could conceive and execute such plans. Each sees the danger in the other's form of thinking, but not in his own. Quinn sees Mauberley's record as "evidence" (52), but Freyberg problematizes the status of evidence itself. When he hits Quinn in the stomach and then denies responsibility for the punch, he seems to be suggesting that the power to assign meaning to evidence, or even to decide what qualifies as evidence, rests with those powerful enough to enforce their assertions.

Throughout the novel, their disputes over how to interpret Mauberley's text highlight the importance of how people read and the questions they bring with them to a text. Quinn looks for beauty and evidence of human survival in the face of death. Freyberg looks for abuses of power. Each finds what he seeks. Each chooses mementos from the war that testify to his chosen focus. Freyberg saves a collection of photographs from the liberation of Dachau. Quinn saves Mauberley's scarf and the broken halves of the Cortot recording of the Schubert Sonata that had sustained Mauberley while he wrote. The novel insists that both sets of memories are not only important but that they are interconnected. Readers cannot choose between these two men and their souvenirs of war without denying what Findley, through Mauberley, is trying to show: how such horror and such beauty could coexist under fascism.

There are two possible ways of explaining fascism as a historical phenomenon. It can be seen as a terrible aberration, or it can be seen as the culmination of the development of Western civilization. I argue that Findley embraces the latter view, interweaving Mauberley's story with that of several others, some historical and some invented. Findley wrote this novel at a time when Western culture was preoccupied with demonizing, eroticizing, or ridiculing fascists—anything to suggest that fascism was not part of contemporary culture. Fascism was effectively cast as a monster without rather than a monster within. Findley's novel shows the human side of fascism, not to make it more palatable but to shock readers once more into seeing how potentially dangerous it may still be as an ideology that can appeal to intelligent and attractive human beings as well as to social outcasts.

Harry Reinhardt, in scenes reminiscent of Ruth's attraction to Race in *The Butterfly Plague,* embodies the sinister power of evil, a "damned beauty" (77), to which Mauberley abases himself. After contracting Harry Reinhardt to kill Harry Oakes, Mauberley licks the blood from the murderer's hands in a consummation of his final fall to moral death. But he escapes from Reinhardt long enough to recover himself through writing his way back into humanity, including the story of his abasement and the pleasure he took in it. When Reinhardt returns to exact the life he has earned through this Faustian bargain, he finds a body but no longer a soul. The true Mauberley now lives in his words on the walls of the hotel, and in the minds and memories of those who read his words. Reinhardt exits the novel like Frankenstein's monster escaping to the north: "And the air was filled with crystal noise and a blowing avalanche into which Harry Reinhardt disappeared" (388–89). Like Frankenstein and his creature and Ruth and Race, the Reinhardt/Mauberley pact shows the fatal cost of dreams of human perfection.

In examining Mauberley's masochistic attraction to Reinhardt, Richard Dellamora argues that *Famous Last Words* is "complicit in an erotics of apocalypse that is both homophobic and homosexual."[16] This dimension of the novel is indeed troubling, but Reinhardt's evil is not in any essential way linked to homosexuality. It is entirely a matter of a vicious male power that destroys anything that gets in its way and that is indifferent to the categorical distinctions that others may make between heterosexual and homosexual. Mauberley is drawn to such power, as Ruth is to Race and Ruth's friend Lisa to her own powerful and rapacious Nazi husband, but Mauberley turns away from that temptation in the end. Mauberley's heroism is that of the collaborator and fearful man who through the act of writing comes so thoroughly to understand his own complicity with evil that he is able eventually to move beyond complicity into resistance.

His heroism is opposed to that of Reinhardt, who is the superman of Nazi dreams. Reinhardt embodies the ultimate Nazi dream of male power; he has become a killing machine bereft of compassion, love, and creativity. He kills Mauberley with an ice pick through the eye because Mauberley's clear-sighted vision no longer either fears or admires what it sees in Reinhardt. The narrator of Mauberley's death is not identified, but whether it is Mauberley himself predicting his death with an astonishing accuracy about the method, or Quinn finishing the story he has become so involved in, or the anonymous narrator of the whole, as seems more likely, the account suggests that this death is not a defeat.

Mauberley's epilogue allegorizes the rise of fascism, a political event, as the eruption of a moral evil from the depths of humanity's past.

Whispering "from the other side of reason" (*Words,* 396), these atavistic urges lie in wait for a humanity that fails to be constantly vigilant. This apocalyptic imagery and allegorical mode prefigure the move away from the realism of the novel toward the fabulistic mode of Findley's next text, *Not Wanted on the Voyage.* This ending, which predicts that evil has only momentarily been defeated and will rise again for another contest, replaces the focus on fresh beginnings that marks the endings of Findley's first two novels.

Modernism on Trial

Robert Ross is brought to trial for treason. Hugh Selwyn Mauberley is unofficially tried through the debates of Quinn and Freyberg, and sentenced to death without a trial by Reinhardt. Findley's radio play, *The Trials of Ezra Pound,* uses actual hearings to embody a metaphorical trial of modernism itself. After the Second World War, the American government held preliminary hearings to determine whether or not Ezra Pound was mentally fit to stand trial for treason because of the fascist propaganda he had broadcast from Italy during the war. Each of these three men embodies an alternative model of heroism based on the courage to adopt unpopular positions within their communities. Their actions force readers to assess their stakes in judging the actions of others.

    None of these men are willing to assume a fully adult responsibility for their behavior, but Robert's compassion is far more attractive a rebellious gesture than Mauberley's fawning on the great or Pound's racist conspiracy theories. This is, of course, Findley's point. It is easy to forgive those with whom one agrees. The test comes in allowing free speech to those whose views are repugnant.

    These men's personal stories assume a symbolic function in Findley's texts. Their stories enact the rise and fall of modernism as a shift in Western thinking that begins with the massive disruptions of the First World War and ends with the dropping of the atomic bombs at the end of the Second World War. Eliot's *Wasteland* and Conrad's *Heart of Darkness* are the modernist texts shadowing Robert's hero's journey into the wasteland, which is the product of Western civilization's drive for unlimited power over the ends of the earth. The stained glass dugout echoes Eliot's poem's conclusion: "These fragments I have shored against my ruins."[17] This could be the manifesto of the novel's narrator as well, as the broken pieces of Robert's story are held as talismans of brightness against the dark collapse of civilization upon itself. In

Famous Last Words and *The Trials of Ezra Pound,* Pound's contradictory life and work symbolize the strengths and weaknesses of modernism as a cultural movement with wide-reaching implications for contemporary society.

Findley's radio play *The Trials of Ezra Pound* was first broadcast in 1990 and published in 1994. The play is set in a Washington, D. C. courtroom in 1946 and is partly based on the transcripts of the actual hearings, although the preface states that the play explores what Pound "did not say at this hearing."[18] Pound emerges as angry, self-centered, and bigoted, a great poet but a weak man. In an interview with Barbara Gabriel, Findley discusses the problem of collaboration that fascinated him in writing *Famous Last Words.* In asking "how artists can ally themselves with the great horrors of their time," Findley suggests that "Mauberley gave in to safety, to wanting to be safe," but that for Pound the safety was the opportunity to indulge his megalomania.[19] The play suggests that Pound's megalomania mirrors that of his place (the mid-Atlantic world linking the United States and Europe) and his era (the twentieth century of modernism's rise and fall).

Findley's play juxtaposes the megalomaniac against the genius and asks if it is possible to separate the two. One of Pound's doctors brings Pound his Mauberley poems and Pound reads, moved by an emotion he had forgotten: "There died a myriad, / And of the best, among them, / For an old bitch—gone in the teeth, / For a botched civilization . . ." (*Trials,* 60). These lines express the insight, the anger, and the sense of betrayal behind *The Wars* and *Famous Last Words.* In its attempt to make a clean break with the past, modernism records and embodies that "botched civilization." Both Robert Ross and Hugh Selwyn Mauberley tried to walk away from their "botched civilization." Pound argues that he tried to fix it.

But even as he argues this, he remains aware of the double meanings of the word fix. When a doctor accuses him of having "fixed ideas," Pound wonders if he means that they are mended or stuck (25). What Pound does not articulate here is a third meaning for fix, which can also mean to rig something to achieve the ends one desires. The play later reveals that the psychiatrists' assessments of Pound's mental lack of fitness to stand trial have been "fixed" in this third sense. Pound himself has earlier implied that he has been imprisoned because he has protested a fix of this nature on the part of his government. Comparing himself to Christ, he asks rhetorically, "Why was Christ crucified?" and answers: "He was crucified for trying to bust a racket! (15–16).

Pound's defense is that he too was trying to bust a racket, to fix a fix, or mend a swindle. He says: "I spoke out, not against my country, but against what my country was doing. Not against my country, but against the conspiracy to bring my country down" (74). The reader may reject Pound's conspiracy theory as paranoia while still insisting on his right to express his views. The test of a democracy is its ability to produce and entertain dissent. Ironically in Findley's play, Pound is now unwillingly part of a genuine American government conspiracy, in which his psychiatrists conspire to have him certified and committed to prevent his trial for treason and the hanging that would surely follow. They wish to preserve the life of one of their greatest poets despite his actions but need to appear be doing their part in denouncing war crimes while the Nuremberg trials are proceeding.

In *The Trials of Ezra Pound* Findley repeats the Quinn/Freyberg debate from *Famous Last Words* through a series of exchanges between his fictional depiction of the real American poet William Carlos Williams, another major figure of American modernism, and an invented Jewish journalist named Albert Deutsch. Deutsch asks: "Should a poet stand trial because of things he says?" Williams's reply is equivocal in the distinction he draws between different degrees of accountability accorded the written and spoken word, and in the assumption he makes that one can separate the poet from the citizen in making such judgments: "Well, he certainly shouldn't stand trial because of what he's written. But for what he's said? A poet, after all, is still a citizen" (17). Later, Williams admits that Pound wrote racist hate literature but argues that he is not on trial for that nor should he be: "We cannot put people on trial because of their opinions" (62). Deutsch is not so sure, but Williams clearly carries authorial endorsement in his pronouncements. Williams remembers Pound as a boy and therefore cannot demonize him as the enemy. He finds it easy to forget that Pound "made his choices" (66) but in balancing "the intellectual horror of the broadcasts, the appalling errors in judgment" against his own assessment that Pound only wanted, "above all else, to be praised" (67), he concludes that one must give Pound the love and praise that he craves. Later, Williams tells Pound that no one forgives him for what he did, but that he is forgiven for what he is (77). What he is remains for the listener to decide. Is he a fallible human being who has made some mistakes or is he actively evil? Is he a genius or a monster or, most troubling and most likely, both? Is he mad, or merely blessed with a greater sensitivity to the paradoxes of contemporary life than the average person?

John Xiros Cooper argues that "[t]he more you know of the personalities and events on which the play is based, the richer you will find Findley's superb enactment."[20] Without such knowledge, the play may seem to lack dramatic action and Pound may emerge as a less sympathetic character than Findley may have wished. As a staging of the complicities and responsibilities of modernism, this play complements the portrait of the era more flamboyantly delineated in *Famous Last Words*. In these texts, the value of literature, like the value of heroes, lies in testing society's limits and putting the assumptions of society itself on trial.

Chapter Four

Endings and Beginnings

Mastery against Mystery

Not Wanted on the Voyage opens with one of the great beginnings of literature: "Everyone knows it wasn't like that."[1] This phrase could be used to
summarize the argument of each of Findley's novels to this point. Con-
trary to the mythologies constructed around the family and war, these
stories show that family life can be harrowing and war is not glamorous.
The hero is the person who dares to point out such truths and not the
person who perpetuates the myths. The cheeky title of *Famous Last
Words* and its origins as an extended improvisation around the fictional
poet-witness of Pound's great modernist poem "Hugh Selwyn Mauberley" prefigures the mode of *Not Wanted on the Voyage* as an extended reply
and rebuttal to the biblical book of Genesis.

Genesis records a series of beginnings and endings: The creation of
Adam and Eve, their expulsion from the garden, the first murder (of
brother by brother), human waywardness and the punishment of the
flood, and the promise of the rainbow that guarantees a new life for the
survivors from Noah's ark to begin again. Findley's first few novels were
preoccupied with predictions of the ending of the world as a holocaust of
fire; here he turns for his organizing principle to the first image of mass
destruction, Noah's flood, although the horror of Noah's sacrificial fires
punctuates the threat of death by drowning with ritual scenes of burning. These scenes of mass destruction are designed to clear away the
mistakes of the past to enable a fresh start. Findley's novel argues that
the best beginnings will be based on remembering rather than drowning or burning away the past. In making such a case, he aligns himself
with a particularly Tory streak in Canadian political ideology that remains
suspicious of notions of progress and modernity, often idealizing a lost
world of the past as offering greater potential for full human development than the contemporary social order.

The novel is composed of a prologue and four books. The prologue
juxtaposes comic and horrific images of "the end of the world" (*Voyage,* 3),
each disguised as a beginning enabled by the embarkation of a voyage

or the ritual of a sacrifice. Book one dramatizes the arrival and then predicts the death through abdication of the novel's God; book two shows
the building and entering of the ark and the death of the Faeries who are
excluded from entering; book three shows life inside the ark, ending
with the simultaneous rape of Emma and the unicorn and the death of
the unicorn; book four shows the aborted revolt of those imprisoned on
the lower decks and the death of Crowe. The novel ends with Mrs.
Noyes, Noah's wife, renewing her refusal of Noah's version of reality
and his vision of the future. In praying for rain, she aligns herself with
everything in the natural world that challenges the fixity of his way of
thinking. He is looking for solid ground on which to found a fresh start;
she prays for rain so that the voyage will never end.

In rewriting Genesis, Findley shows the narrative of origins as the site
of a power struggle. The voices excluded from Genesis have their say
here. Women, children, workers (invoked through the descriptor "the
lower orders" and through the depiction of Emma's family as English
peasants), animals, and creatures from folklore (Lucifer, the Faeries,
demons, dragons, and unicorns) are all presented as interested partici-
pants in Noah's attempt at establishing his version of events and his
control over events as dominant. By contesting the official version of the
story, Findley redefines Noah's new world order not as a divinely sanctioned origin for a new world, as the Bible would have it, but as a strate-
gically grasped beginning. In distinguishing origins from beginnings, I
am relying on Edward Said's explanation that "beginning and beginning-
again are historical, whereas origins are divine."[2] Findley's opening words
in this novel dramatize the challenge that history poses to myth as a
competing system of interpretation for understanding and recording
human actions. *The Wars* and *Famous Last Words* used myth to challenge
the silences left by historical modes of describing human action; this
novel reverses the process, using the voice of history to challenge the
silences of myth.

For Findley, endings and beginnings are intimately related. As a Canadian, he knows that the beginnings of Canada as a nation demanded the
ending of the rule of the First Nations in that disputed geographical
space. His first two novels imagined a return to Eden for the survivors of
their holocausts. In *Not Wanted on the Voyage,* as the title implies, he imagines the world that Noah has jettisoned to enable the triumph of Noah's
ark and the establishment of a world more tightly under Noah's control.
The novel begins by asking potentially sacrilegious questions: What was
left behind to be swallowed by the flood? What is the cost of survival and

on what terms has it been negotiated? Is the present order of things worth the price? Noah's wife, Mrs. Noyes, is aligned with the asking of such questions and with the world left behind; Noah is aligned with the suppression of such questions and the world that triumphs as a result of the flood. Her world, of respect for nature and communion with all living things, is replaced by his world, of rules and edicts, of conquest and destruction. Her rebellion against her husband parallels Lucifer's earlier rebellion against God. Each of them champions mystery against those who wish to wield a mastery over the universe.

Her world is allied with the magical sign the Faeries give her before their destruction, the sign of infinity that Findley reproduces at the beginning of each section of text. The infinity sign promises the endless fertility of the creative imagination and the inexhaustible diversity of forms of life beyond the human. Noah's world is marked by two signs he has produced to fool his audience into thinking he has access to divine power: the paper whale predicting the flood and the rainbow promising its abatement. These signs signal his hostility to diversity and his intolerance of interpretative play. Noah's signs function unidirectionally and can mean only one thing: what he says they mean. In contrast, the infinity sign, by its very nature, encourages multiple interpretations. Indeed, closure is the only thing it disallows.

Findley sets his retelling of the biblical fable in the Edwardian period at the height of the British Empire, with "a band playing *Rule Britannia!* and *Over the Sea to Skye.* Flags and banners and a booming cannon . . . like an excursion" (*Voyage,* 3). The juxtapositions are both incongruously comic and pointed in the analogies they suggest between the Judeo-Christian story of a world divided between the lost and the saved and the justifying ideologies of an imperialism that divided the world into the colonizers and the colonized. Helen Tiffin provides the most extended analysis of *Not Wanted on the Voyage* as a postcolonial interrogation of imperial power, its ambivalences, its justificatory mythologies, and its destructive heritage.[3] As Donna Pennee points out in her book-length study of this text, it is also possible to expand this reading to identify a revisionary strategy that questions the philosophical underpinnings behind the different modes of oppression whose legacy we still struggle with today: received notions about prescribed relations between women and men, between humans and other species, and between humans and their natural environment.[4]

Cecilia Martell argues that "Findley addresses the ways in which contemporary society tries desperately to 'normalize' people, social practices, gender, religion, dogma, and exegesis through his placement of humorous elements in stark juxtaposition to horror and history" in *Not Wanted on the Voyage*.[5] She expresses disappointment that most criticism focuses on these serious themes to the neglect of the "camp humour" through which they are often expressed. As she points out, in rebutting Genesis the opening lines of the novel also record the reader's complicity with what "everyone knows," a form of knowledge as common sense that this novel questions through its use of camp. Whereas Tiffin stresses the imperial context evoked in the novel's opening scene, Martell concentrates attention on its incongruity and silliness from a contemporary perspective, yet the challenge is to see how these elements work together to force a fresh perspective on the unquestioned assumptions of common knowledge. By focusing on the campiness and bad taste of the imperial, Martell implies that contemporary readers have moved beyond all that, yet Findley's novel demands that readers recognize their own complicities in similar ventures today. The novel's anachronisms reject the view of history as progress, one of the underpinning ideological assumptions of imperialism, to insist instead on the timeliness of the novel's concerns with the establishment of a new world order.

The camp perspective of the opening scene establishes Noah as ridiculous, but as Martell points out, the horror of the following scene reminds us of the very real power to do harm that this man still wields. It is hard to keep laughing at a man who causes the sheep to lose their ability to sing, denies the Faeries asylum, throws the demons overboard, and massacres his own children. Noah's rape and murder of the unicorn as a means of raping his daughter-in-law Emma is the final, most horrific act that signals his abuse of power through a misguided notion of manhood that equates destructive violence with virility. This is the turning point of the novel, the event that precipitates the uprising of the forces below against Noah's monstrous regime. The equivalent of Robert's rape in *The Wars,* this scene takes the betrayal of trust one step further as Noah disclaims his violence, pretending a scientific objectivity and a helpful intent, and hypocritically concluding: "I have only done my duty as a father" (*Voyage,* 265). Emma's screams go unattended. A "holy purpose" is manufactured for the unicorn's death (271).

Against the betrayal of his rape, Robert renews his links to life through consolidating his fellowship with the horses in *The Wars.* The intimate bonds between the human and animal worlds below deck provide similar comfort for Emma, but they also provide what Robert did not have: a shared sense of political will to act for change. Just as the stained glass dugout provides Robert with companions who share his love of beauty, his compassion for others, and his sense of humor, so the world below decks provides its prisoners with these resources. But it also provides the catalyzing leadership of the iconoclastic Lucy.

The power of laughter as a weapon of resistance is most effectively wielded by Lucy, the novel's central camp character. S/he is self-described as "[s]even-foot-five; and every inch a queen" (249). Findley follows Blake in identifying Lucifer as the radical hero of Milton's *Paradise Lost,* but he pushes the concept further to redefine Lucy/Lucifer's heroism as that of the transvestite performer who, "with his/her jet black hair, powdered white face, and kimono, is figured as an Onna Gata from Japanese Kabuki theatre—that ideal distillation of the feminine that is always performed by a man."[6] Although the Archangel Michael refers to his brother Lucifer as "he," the text refers to Lucy as "she." Michael argues that although his brother is not a man, he is a male. Lucy responds with a shrug: "I like dressing up" (*Voyage,* 107). Technically, as an angel Lucy is not subject to human gender distinctions, but her function here seems to be to confuse such distinctions. As an angel who has chosen to align herself with the human world, rejecting God and his heaven to marry Ham, Noah's gentle and thoughtful son, Lucy crosses borders that are usually closed to crossing. For that reason I refer to this creature as s/he to indicate the instability s/he refuses to resolve.

Lucy punctures the pretensions of the powerful through playful wit but can also unleash a more terrible destructive force against those s/he wishes to destroy. S/he kills Emma's dog, Barky, because s/he is afraid of dogs, proving the novel's thesis that most violence stems from fear. Lucy's beauty has its sinister side: Her fingers are webbed, the wolves fear her, and s/he smells of sulfur. In their innocence, Mrs. Noyes and Ham read Lucy's appearance as her reality, but Mrs. Noyes's cat, Mottyl, is wiser. She finds this creature "odd" and dangerous (59), although later she is pleased that Lucy is on their side.

Lucy's aesthetic is reminiscent of the stained glass dugout in *The Wars.* Like Devlin, she is devoted to fragility: "Lucy's greatest fascination seemed to be with the outcasts and the pariahs, the strangely formed and excessively delicate" (275). But it is Lucy's hybrid identity that most effectively challenges the binary way of thinking that distinguishes Noah and that is encapsulated in the no/yes division of his last name, "Noyes." Lucy's crime in heaven was asking "[w]hy?" (108). Neither God nor Michael think this a legitimate question. They want obedience, not thinking subjects. Noah divides the world of his ark into the upper deck, populated by those who say yes to his plans (his sons Shem and Japeth, and Hannah, Shem's wife and Noah's mistress) and the lower deck, to which he consigns those who have refused to assent to his vision (his wife; her cat, Mottyl; Ham and Lucy; and Emma, Japeth's wife). Members of this latter group do not always say no, but they always ask why before they make up their minds. In thinking about Ham, Lucy remembers that "[a]ll his answers were *yes* and *no*—and all his questions were equally terse: *why*? He would say —and *what for*?" (338). Although it is tempting for readers to accept Noah's divisions of the novel's world into two halves and simply reverse the moral evaluations he has assigned to them, such a reading would undermine the novel's more complex message, which rejects the kind of thinking that separates an "us" from a "them." At a philosophical level these divisions enabled colonialism and fascism. To the extent that they are fundamental to Western civilization, they need to be rethought.

The novel's deployment of "yes" and "no" may seem paradoxical. One way of reading the novel is to see it as the story of Mrs. Noyes's education in how to say "no." At the beginning of the novel, although she wanted to deny Noah the sacrifices he craved, Mrs. Noyes "could not even say No" (26). She enacts her refusal, fleeing Noah's ark, entering the forbidden orchard, and rejoicing in her brief freedom. She becomes an ark for the Faeries, carrying them across the river to temporary safety. But she fails to save Lotte, whom Japeth murders on his father's orders. By the end of the novel she is able to say her "no" out loud, even if it is beyond Noah's hearing (352). In the context of the novel's struggle, her "no" to Noah is a "yes" to life in all its mystery and diversity. Her "no" is further from Noah's "no" than any "yes" could be. The death of the Faeries at the end of book two repeats the horror of the fire at Alvarez Canyon in *The Butterfly Plague,* when creatures fighting for their lives meet the closed walls of a structure that "takes on a voice. And the voice said: *no*" (193). Noah's "no" is a closed door; Mrs. Noyes's "no" is an opening onto something new.

Some readers have been surprised that despite this novel's open contesting of apparent biblical truths, such as the omnipotence and goodness of God, the perfection of heaven, and the righteousness of Noah, Christians have not generally objected to this book and it has not attracted the anger with which many in the Muslim community greeted Salman Rushdie's *Satanic Verses.* Indeed, many readers seem to enjoy Findley's portrayal of God as a dirty old man with food in his beard who sucks lozenges and trails flies, and to accept without question the novel's characterization of heaven as a Gulag where "a person's clothes were always at the cleaners. *Being improved.* . . . Or else, the *person* was at the cleaners, being improved . . ." (339). This positive response suggests that Findley's critique of certain elements in the Old Testament story of Noah's Flood can be assimilated very easily into the standard Christian belief system, which sees the New Testament story of Christ's message of love correcting and superseding the Old Testament focus on judgment and the law. By opposing the Christian forgiveness and love of Mrs. Noyes and her supporters with the Old Testament wrath and rigidity of Noah and his God, Findley may be seen as an advocate of true Christian values. His attack on hypocrites such as Noah and the old pretender god he has fashioned in his own image can easily be seen as pro-Christian rather than anti-Christian.

The novel's stand on abortion and eugenics adds strength to this view. Noah wishes to kill imperfect children. The rift between Noah and his wife has initially been caused by his inability to accept the fact that he carries the genetic imperfection that has given them what the novel calls "Lotte-children," a description that humanizes the clinical, assigning individuality to a condition that others might label "developmentally delayed," "disabled," or "differently abled." Japeth's lost twin was one such child. Noah has engineered Emma's marriage to Japeth because the existence of Emma's sister, Lotte, means that she will be blamed if their union produces another "Lotte-child." Mrs. Noyes loves these children and tries to save their lives. Her husband destroys them.

Theoretically, Lucy may pose the biggest problem for a Christian reading of this text, but in fact s/he is portrayed in a manner that makes her closer to Christ than to the devil of traditional Christian representations. Like Christ, s/he has abandoned heaven to take on human shape and submit to the sorrows of mortality. S/he sustains and defends the novel's most likable characters and teases and humiliates the nasty ones. A survivor of the "holocaust in heaven," s/he is not able to prevent the "holocaust on earth," but s/he does contribute to the resistance (110). Lucy performs the novel's one true miracle, the ceremony in which the collective below deck is able to remember the unicorn alive for a few precious moments (280–81). This ceremony most closely resembles the method of Findley's memoir, *Inside Memory,* where he recites the stories of his friends who have died to renew their living through remembrance. Afterwards, Lucy speaks of why s/he left heaven. S/he "wanted difference" (382), and s/he wanted salvation for all, not just the chosen few.

S/he is still seeking a world "where darkness and light are reconciled" (284), and where s/he would be free to be *"whoever I wish to be"* (282). Lucy's "promised land" (282) sounds much like the promised land of America. It is hard to imagine Christians protesting such a vision, despite the apparent unorthodoxy of assigning such views to a campy character named Lucifer who dresses as Lucy.

George Woodcock suggests that Findley's parable fits within the tradition of gnostic writing, in which "Buddha, Zoroaster, Jesus, and Mani . . . were variously identified by the Gnostics as messengers from the world of light. It does not stretch the pattern very far to see among them the Creator's original antagonist, Lucifer."[7] Even Lucifer's assumption of a female role can be seen as part of posing an alternative vision to the patriarchal rule of Yahweh and Noah, he argues. I find Mervyn Nicholson's argument that this novel participates in an "infernal tradition" that is sociopolitical in emphasis much more convincing. Nicholson argues that this tradition reads the Bible subversively to liberate "a subtext of social oppression, mental repression."[8] Far from attacking Christianity, such a tradition "attacks the complex of sociocultural assumptions" in which the Christianity of the author's time is embedded (Nicholson, 104).

I have explained that I see Lucy/Lucifer as a transvestic figure of problematized gender who is neither male nor female but ontologically other (technically a rebel angel) and specifically a rebel against the dominance of "the world of light." In my view, Lucy's hybridity signals the novel's opposition to Noah's binary thinking. To call the novel a "gnostic parable" is to see the novel continuing to operate within binary structures that have merely flipped the traditional associations assigned to each half of the binary. By having Lucy seek a world where light and darkness are valued equally, by showing Mrs. Noyes choosing to remain with Noah while disputing his views, and by recording Mottyl's refusal to hate Noah for blinding her and killing her children, Findley throws binary ways of thinking into question.

Mottyl's perception of events is crucial. Animals provide a privileged locus of otherness in this novel. Findley regularly uses a person's attitude toward animals as an indicator of character, but in *Not Wanted on the Voyage* he goes one step further to make animals perceiving centers of consciousness and important characters in their own right. The friendship between Mottyl and Crowe remains a touchstone of value, and Crowe is the hero of the text in sacrificing her life for the greater good of her friends. Japeth, who wants to be a hero, becomes a villain because he cannot think of heroism as anything but violence. Japeth had set out on a quest "to find his manhood once and for all—and, returning, to slay the dragon of Emma's virginity and kill the giant of his shame. But things had not worked out that way" (*Voyage,* 23). As a result of his near-fatal encounter with the Ruffian King and the horror of the canni-bal feast "on the road to Baal and Mammon" (79), Japeth returns home, literally "blue" and more desperate than ever. In a scene that recalls Fagan's distinction between the shot and the shout at the end of *The Wars,* Japeth fulfills his deadly equation of virility with violence. The dolphins greeting the ark with friendly delight are labeled evil pirates by Noah, and Japeth's deadly blow killing the friendly dolphins ensures that Noah's interpretation will prevail over that of Mrs. Noyes: "The whole visage was a message of joy and greeting. But in that moment of recognition, as Mrs. Noyes and the creature looked at one another and smiled—Japeth's sword descended—swiftly and fatally" (237).

After Noah's rape and murder of the unicorn, Mottyl thinks of Noah's experiments and edicts and almost adds the phrase "evil ways" but stops herself and then wonders why she has stopped (279). She runs through a damning catalog of his evil actions, but at the end of the list she still refuses to pass judgment, thinking instead: "What could a per-son truly know . . . ?" (279). Noah has always judged too quickly; Mot-tyl would prefer to suspend judgment. Her decision shows her greater wisdom and maturity, and warns readers to avoid falling into Noah's trap. In this novel, it is the half-blind cat who truly sees into the heart of things. Denied her physical vision (in one eye) by Noah's experiments, she develops her spiritual insight.

The novel's epigraph, taken from Canadian poet Phyllis Webb's "Leaning," seems to refer to the intimate companionship of Mottyl and Mrs. Noyes, two survivors of the various holocausts that Noah has unleashed on his world: "And you, are you still here / tilting in this stranded ark / blind and seeing in the dark." Findley told Barbara Gabriel that "[t]he original story was about a cat on a farm in southern Ontario in 1910 and about a blizzard" (Gabriel, "Masks," 31). The cat remains, but the blizzard has become the Flood and the specifics of the Canadian place and time have disappeared.

I have argued elsewhere that the Canadian perspective survives in the particular attitude to place and to change that Findley advocates in this novel.[9] What the Hartz thesis terms a "tory streak" in Canada's ideologi-cal makeup has always been a nebulous concept privileging the United Empire Loyalist heritage, suspicious of individualism but tolerant of dis-sent.[10] In *Lament for a Nation,* George Grant argues that Canada is in danger of abandoning its Tory identity, which he defines as a belief that "public order and tradition, in contrast to freedom and experiment, were central to the good life."[11] The Tory myth draws on a postlapsarian Old Testament view of the world, which *Not Wanted on the Voyage* ostensibly questions but ultimately, in some key respects, confirms. Arthur Kroker summarizes the discourse of what he calls "the tory ego in North America: lamentation not emancipation; historical fatalism not collective political struggle; contemplation not engagement; and equivocation not pragmatism."[12] What Kroker defines negatively can be defined more positively as a greater focus on the cost of change disguised as progress. *Not Wanted on the Voyage* itemizes those costs and finds them too high. The novel voices sharp suspicion of what Noah terms progress. Just as Canada rejected a revolution in favor of incremental change, so Findley argues that change is best achieved by building on the strengths of the past rather than annihilating it. On the whole, the argument is convincingly presented. Mrs. Noyes and Mottyl are among his most sympathetic characters. Yet the novel's romanticization of Emma's peasant family as a locus of salt of the earth values and its privileging of Lucy's aristocratic manner suggest that the class alliances of such views conform to certain aspects of modernism (such as its contestation of modernity defined as the rule of a middle class lacking in taste and imagination) even as the thrust of the argument contests the need for a clean break with the past.

The dominant mood is elegiac: So many wonders have been lost from the world, so many lives extinguished, and for what end? To bolster Noah's ego and solidify his power. Such a goal is not worth the price. It is looking backward at what has been lost that drives the vision of a possibly better future for those who plan the revolt of the lower orders. Mottyl's death song celebrates the wonder, the detail, and the mystery of a world "that was: of the world that could never be again. In blind Mottyl's mind was the last whole vision of the world before it drowned." The rhythms of "Gone, now. / under / Forever" (*Voyage,* 333) repeat the rhythms of Crowe's death: "*Bam!* / The board hit her. / Crowe" (327). Here is where the emotional power of this text resides: in its elegy for a lost way of living and a lost way of seeing. In part, it is an elegy for childhood itself; in part, for a lost sense of community.

The contrast between the selfish individualism of Noah's group above deck and the cooperative spirit among the people and animals below deck is evidenced in the difference in spirit between Noah's banishment of his wife and one son from his table and the elephant One Tusk's saving of Mottyl and her kittens, complete strangers to him, with the wise words, "We are all in this together—and we must do what we can do" (229). Out of this philosophy comes a vision of the garrison world of below-deck as a kind of peaceable kingdom. These are two of Northrop Frye's most resonant images for the old Tory Canadian community: the garrison, because literally the land was founded on forts that were as much prisons shutting people in from the land and its first inhabitants as they were shelters from the dangers perceived to lurk beyond the walls; and the peaceable kingdom, an image of a world where peace and not war would be the norm. It is hell to be trapped in this dark, enclosed space, yet there is the comfort of the cradle in the warmth they create together. Despite the intermixing of the species, they are safe together. Mrs. Noyes can lie down to sleep in the den of the bear. She need not fear dragons or snakes. Sharing "the same jailor," she thinks, you "learn to survive together in ways the uncaged world would never think of" (251). This positive vision of a human community coextensive with the animal and supernatural worlds is founded on the values associated with the lost, drowned world, and not with Noah's new one.

Mrs. Noyes's experiences in learning to conquer her fear lead her to conclude that "[c]ruelty was fear in disguise" and "fear itself was nothing more than a failure of the imagination" (252). Such a belief enables compassion but makes fighting a defined enemy difficult. When Ham tells Lucy he does not want to kill his father or his brothers, Lucy responds that they cannot win unless they can at least entertain the possibility of killing for their beliefs. How does one fight absolute ruthlessness without becoming ruthless oneself? When forced to kill the sacrificial lamb at the beginning of the novel, Ham cuts himself while cutting the lamb, sharing in the pain he is forced to inflict. Robert's maiming in *The Wars* after his acts of murder seems to take on a similar function. Only through some kind of self-sacrifice can violence become the remedy for violence, but Ham is committed to finding a nonviolent way to achieve his alternative vision of social order. Laughter and words can work as weapons and witnessing, countering Noah's edicts with all the resources of the imagination. Noah's motto is "mastery by whatever means" (239). To combat such ruthlessness, Findley offers his most lyrical, tender, and funniest celebration of the powers of the imagination.

Memory as Asylum and Agency

Inside Memory: Pages from a Writer's Workbook constructs a fragmented memoir of a writer's life that contributes to the mask of the writer while sheltering the man. The book is constructed around the doubled notion of memory as a shelter from the ravages of the world and as the necessary prerequisite for taking action in that world. Just as Findley's short story collection *Stones* begins and ends in ritual ceremonies for the dead, so *Inside Memory* begins and ends with the thematic exploration of remembering as a means for transforming an ending into a beginning. Findley locates his beginning on Remembrance Day, November 11, the day reserved to remember the war dead of two world wars. As so often in this book, he situates his own commentary on a subject through his reading of another writer's handling of the theme. In writing that "Chekhov discovered the dramatic value of memory" (*Memory*, 3), Findley indirectly records his own ambition to do the same. His anatomy of memory includes describing it as "[c]athartic," "purgative," "a form of hope" (4), a form of identity (5), and, above all, an affirmation of community and survival. For Findley, memory is the strongest form of imaginative empathy: "Remembrance is more than honouring the dead. Remembrance is joining them—being one with them in memory" (7).

He situates his final chapter in Mount Pleasant Cemetery, "city of the dead" (264), a gardened space in the heart of urban Toronto, full of the life of the natural world. This is where Findley tried to learn to drive and where he abandoned the effort, a comic interlude with a certain symbolic significance given that his efforts to reverse have created "scars" on the Massey Mausoleum: a fitting monument to Findley's family's imbrication in the privilege and authority of a Canadian tradition (264; 267). Findley's failure as a driver symbolically marks his success as a rebel, deviating from the family heritage to create his own destiny as a writer suspicious of institutional structures. Vines hide what Findley proudly thinks of as his "sins against the Masseys" (267), but Findley here parades his ambivalence about this heritage for the public record.

His memoir narrates his turn away from the car, symbol of the technological dominance of space in the twentieth century, and his abandonment of the city for the green space of a farm deep in the country, where his family had its preurban roots. He has named this farm in honor of Chekhov's *Cherry Orchard*, that classic embodiment of nostalgia for a vanishing way of life, unaware, he insists, until afterward that the name he has chosen, "Stone Orchard," is local parlance for a graveyard. In this careful choice of details revealed, Findley creates the mystique of the writer and of the space from which he writes.

Just as the memoir records a series of births as each novel is created and sent out into the world, followed by the void of emptiness before beginning again, so the rest of Findley's final chapter becomes a series of obituaries for family members, writers, and other artists he has known. Like Lucy remembering the unicorn alive in *Not Wanted on the Voyage*, he remembers each character alive for a time before moving on to the next. Each of their special qualities reveals something more about the man who loved them and now remembers them. The final section reprints his address to the Philosophical Society of Trent University under the general heading "My Final Hour." Here Findley discusses the first great crisis of his life at the age of 15, his discovery that others changed their attitudes toward him when he revealed his sexual orientation, something he had accepted without question in himself from an early age. He explains: "The subject at hand is not my sexual orientation. . . . The subject here is other people's lack of reconciliation to the person I was. The whole person" (304). Findley's work mocks and rages against such ostracism, but even more importantly, it enables readers afraid of difference to experience its mystery through the acts of reconciliation that a book can create. Findley explains his own shock of recognition in seeing the emotions he felt embodied in Shakespeare's Richard, Duke of Gloucester. Ironically, in finding this character who insists "*I am myself alone*" (306), Findley discovers that he is not alone and that he has been seen and acknowledged through Shakespeare's art. He finds a complementary revelation in the discovery of the photographs of Dachau in Ivan Moffat's Hollywood home: "This is the worst and the hardest of reconciliations: the one that forces you into the company of murderers" (311). This is the closest Findley comes to articulating his aesthetic. In believing that the goal of art is reconciliation, the artist cannot compromise in what he shows. The "writer is a witness" who must remain "naive," retaining the capacity for wonder at "the way of the world" (313). If he is true to this task, then imagination can save the world (314). This is the credo with which he ends the book, with a call to fight despair by facing it down. Art provides the resources for imagining otherwise, for finding the strength in the survivals from earlier mass destructions, from the Ice Age to the holocaust, to follow Lucy's example in seeking a better world for the future. Out of endings, to create new beginnings.

This is Findley's public reading of his own work. It is persuasive and inspiring, but in its privileging of reconciliation as ending and beginning, it neglects other aspects of his achievement that are equally compelling, if more troubling. Each of Findley's endings gives voice or visibility to things that evade the novels' concluding reconciliations: to what remains irreconcilable, outside resolution, outside full articulation. In the endings these are images of dread, but in Findley's humor they erupt as anarchic elements of promise and possibility. In choosing not to remember these aspects of his vision, Findley engages in a strategic forgetting that is as significant as what he enshrines in memory. The public persona is more solemn, more conforming to public respectabilities, and more consistently uplifting in tone than are the literary texts themselves.

In an article that argues the "transgressive textuality " of *Inside Memory* as photographic life-writing, Lorraine York asserts that Findley has refused "to write an autobiography which promises, and claims to deliver, disclosure of a self."[13] I want to modify this slightly. Findley refuses disclosure of a previously hidden, private self, but he diligently constructs a public persona that closely links a particular self to a privileged interpretation of the texts that pass under the name of that self. The Findley constructed in *Inside Memory* authorizes the works and is authorized by them.

The middle of the book moves chronologically, recording the steps Findley takes on his way to such an affirmation. Most of the chapter titles are the titles of his novels, key steps along this journey, but one records the importance of the place "Stone Orchard" in his life and another reprints his dialogue with William Whitehead about his life and work, "Alice Drops Her Cigarette on the Floor." The pattern is articulated in the second chapter, "From Stage to Page": "People are the landscape of memory" (*Memory*, 11). Just as Findley's novels center on character, so does the memoir, but the characters in *Inside Memory* are the people Findley meets, who serve as mentors or models for his writing.

The book proceeds as a series of little epiphanies, with each character showing, in his or her own way, the importance of being oneself and of believing in oneself, not as a liberty but as a responsibility. The final interlude involves Findley's Los Angeles friendship with a fly, whose drowning he takes as a message to get out of town and return to the country. The book is full of such images of whimsical humor, so that the cumulative effect is of a varied, full life, packed with the stories of others and the questions they pose for the self.

As a collection of fragments of various kinds of writing meant for different occasions—diary entries, speeches, interviews, anecdotes, obituaries—the book becomes the equivalent of the stained glass dugout in *The Wars*, or Lilah's talismans in *Headhunter*, or Minna's pocketbook full of her totems in "A Bag of Bones": a repository of symbols that resonate

with memory and the power to conjure life itself. Like the novels, stories, and plays, Findley's memoir invites readers to enter the space he
has created to honor the dead, a rival mausoleum to outlast that of the
Masseys in the graveyard of Toronto's elite. This is a space where time is
altered and ultimately conquered, if only momentarily.

Chapter Five
Evil Empires

My title, "evil empires," carries with it the whiff of melodramatic conspiracy theories, the end of the Cold War rhetoric, and, for those old enough to remember, an echo of United States president Ronald Reagan's characterization of the Soviet Union in the language of moral conflict popularized by the Hollywood *Star Wars* movies. These are the contexts evoked in *The Telling of Lies* and *Headhunter*. Findley's writing regularly combines two of the most important representational systems in contemporary North America: religion and psychiatry. His imagery consistently relocates the evil empire from a nation-state outside a nation's borders to identify an enemy within. Race follows Ruth to America in *The Butterfly Plague*, but what he represents was already there in her father George's murder of the Chinese-American workman. Robert's enemies in *The Wars* are not the Germans but his fellow officers. Hugh Selwyn Mauberley's biggest enemy is himself in *Famous Last Words*. In *The Telling of Lies* and *Headhunter*, the evil empire still refers to the betrayal of the authority vested in those assigned the responsibility of leadership, but its evil lies in the complicitous relations developed among the institutions of business, government, and psychiatry.

Findley first introduces the idea of scientific experimentation on living beings as torture in *The Butterfly Plague*, when Ruth realizes that her endurance as a swimmer in icy water is setting the standard for further Nazi experiments on the victims of the camps. In *Not Wanted on the Voyage*, Dr. Noyes's experiments on the cat Mottyl's kittens, killing them all, are contrasted with the humane, scientific explorations of his much more rational son, Ham. Although these are horrific examples of an abuse of power that both victimizes and radicalizes Ruth and Mottyl, the suffering witnesses to inhumanity in these novels, these experiments are not the central focus of attention. In *The Telling of Lies* and *Headhunter*, Findley addresses the responsibilities of the pharmaceutical industries and the psychiatric establishment to their patients and to the societies in which they operate more directly. In their ability to wield unquestioned power, they are seen as the new face of empire.

In *The Telling of Lies,* the industrialist Calder Maddox claims that "he owned half the world and rented the other half."[1] His "empire" is rumored to be founded on various chemicals, from "Agent Orange to Byblow B" (*Lies,* 13). Besides the weapons of war, he manufactures mood-altering drugs used in psychiatry, such as "Maddonix to put them to sleep and Maddonite to wake them up. And Maddoxin to calm them in between" (11). The name of the drug implies an addiction that drives its takers mad. Although Maddox is implicitly described as having a "genius for evil" (13), the doctors who use his drugs to alter people's memories receive the brunt of the novel's anger. The mystery at the heart of *The Telling of Lies* turns out not to be Maddox's murder on the beach in Maine but the secret story of CIA-funded experiments on psychiatric patients in Montreal during the Cold War, experiments conducted by a fictional Dr. Allan Potter on Canadian citizens with the knowledge of the Canadian government. Dr. Potter is modeled on the actual Dr. Ewan Cameron, an eminent psychiatrist under whom Montreal's Allan Institute acquired the largest psychiatric research budget in Canada during the 1950s and early 1960s. He died in 1967. In 1977, the CIA funding of his research was revealed and in 1980 several of his former patients launched a highly publicized lawsuit against the U.S. government.[2] The fictional Dr. Potter's experiments, like those of Dr. Cameron, involve "reprogramming" the human brain, erasing memory, and installing new messages. The action of the novel takes place entirely in the United States and the novel's central character and narrator, Vanessa Van Horne, is an American citizen. These facts underline the permeability of national borders under contemporary global capitalism. A further irony reveals that the Canadian experiments are seen as minor within the larger context of Maddox's involvements with several United States government departments; they are literally the tip of the iceberg and not sufficiently important to risk drawing attention to the rest of the empire. What seems central to Meg (Maddox's murderer) and to Canadians generally is revealed as peripheral to the new American empire. Vanessa discovers evil in high places in her own American government.

Headhunter resituates Conrad's *Heart of Darkness* within the practices of the fictional Parkin Institute of Psychiatric Research in Toronto during the 1980s, where experiments with a new drug, Obedian, continue under the supervision of the power-hungry psychiatrist-in-chief, Kurtz. As in *Lies,* the name of the drug signals an interest in creating obedient slaves out of formerly active citizens to enable the smoother running not just of Kurtz's own private empire but of the larger political structures that depend on his collaboration to stifle dissent. But Kurtz, like Maddox, is also involved in a variety of other experiments in mind control. He has followed Dr. Cameron's research on *"psychic driving"* at Montreal's Allan Memorial Institute (called by their real names here), and his own related experiments with white noise are seen as *"the great white hope of sleep therapy"* (*Headhunter,* 118). This phrase connects the civilizational alibi of imperialism that disguised a quest for "naked power" (which Kurtz sees as essentially male) with Kurtz's research in psychiatry (119). The empire of healing becomes an empire of destruction just as the empire of Western civilization enabled racism, economic exploitation, and cultural devastation. Findley's recurrent interest in abuses of power moves in these novels from the level of the individual within the family to the level of collective action within the community, a shift first signaled in the dynamics of *Not Wanted on the Voyage,* where the lower orders collaborate in their revolt against Noah and his supporters.

Erasing Memory

The Telling of Lies is subtitled "A Mystery" and the novel won the Edgar Award for the best original paperback from the Mystery Writers of America. From his first novel, Findley has demonstrated an interest in the codes and conventions of genre and an impulse to disturb them in his fiction. Catherine Hunter analyzes the way Findley sets in motion the contradictory meanings of the word "mystery," how he approaches it as rule-bound genre on the one hand and as indicator of the uncanny or inexplicable, of everything that resists articulation, codification, and resolution or "solving," on the other. She argues that *"The Telling of Lies* unravels the rhetoric on which the whole genre is based. For at the heart of the mystery is the eradication of mystery . . . an insane desire for sanity."[3] In other words, this novel resituates the struggle that *Not Wanted on the Voyage* poses between Noah's insane pursuit of mastery, which must destroy life's mystery, and Mrs. Noyes's desire to protect and appreciate the mysterious on its own terms, transferring the telling from the genre of the biblical parable into the language of the detective novel. In political terms, Noah is the novel's revolutionary, willing to throw out everything from the past to install his vision of what ought to be, whereas Mrs. Noyes is the conservative who mourns the loss of everything that Noah makes disappear. In destroying mystery, Noah also destroys memory. With the dying of Mottyl, the full sensory experience of the beautiful world drowned in the flood is lost to the world, save for the preservation provided it in Findley's text. *The Telling of Lies* is more directly an inquiry into the nature and importance of memory, in some ways the fictional companion to Findley's memoir, *Inside Memory*.

When Vanessa Van Horne, Findley's detective narrator, discovers the reason for Maddox's murder, she uncovers a motive of revenge for a plot that seems much more terrible than the murder itself because it is authorized by a government and a medical establishment that should be safeguarding rather than risking the lives of the people it has been elected to protect. This plot involves obliterating people's memories in an insane attempt to create a tabula rasa for them to begin again, much as the European settler immigrants to North America created the alibi of the tabula rasa in denial of the history of the continent before their arrival to enable their own fresh beginning. The moral outrage at this discovery seems especially acute because the story is based on actual experiments conducted on real people by Dr. Ewan Cameron at the Allan Memorial Institute in Montreal, who is presented as Dr. Allan Potter in this novel but as himself in *Headhunter*. Cameron's techniques of "psychic driving," which the CIA eventually decided were of little interest to them, seem to have been a genuinely misguided attempt to heal through thought control, but they reveal a terrible lack of imagination at the heart of the drive for perfection that may be more frightening and more difficult to combat than outright brainwashing for social control. It is easier to imagine a conspiracy created by monsters than to be forced to see that idealist impulses can lead to terrible ends. Vanessa, needing to see a conspiracy and find someone to blame, discovers instead her own complicity in what has happened.

The horrible irony of the book lies in the dilemma Vanessa faces when she learns of the experiments. If she exposes the secret, she may expose the murderer to a punishment Vanessa believes she does not deserve (although it is more likely she would simply expose herself to silencing), but if she does not tell, she has joined the other side in their plot to obliterate true memories of the past. The true crime, she comes to believe, is not the murder of Calder Maddox after all, but the cover-up that led to his murder and now necessitates the denial of the fact of the murder itself. Although Vanessa makes her choice to join in the telling of lies by hiding the truth, the novel leaves the rightness of her decision, and the reasons for it, open to question.

Because the story of the novel is told in the first person through Vanessa's diary, there is no contending voice to balance hers, but her defensiveness about her decision and her recognition of the double bind in which it places her allows an opening for doubt. She writes: "I admit I have joined my enemies. I am prepared to do what they have done: even to use their weapons. I do not admit that this is wrong. I would ask whoever questions this to tell me what is right" (*Lies,* 359). Furthermore, through her diary, she makes public her decision to keep the secret hidden. Her writing tells what her actions will deny. By articulating this challenge to "whoever questions," and by concluding that "[s]omeone sold us out—but only when we ceased to pay attention," (359), she challenges the reader to pay attention and not allow the telling of lies to continue without dispute.

Hunter explains that "the mystery is a double narrative, reading the story of the present (the detection) in order to tell the story of the past (the crime)" (Hunter, 99). *The Wars* plays this structure against the conventions of historical fiction to problematize what has officially been labeled Robert's "crime," renaming it an act of heroism and locating the true "crime" elsewhere, in the rape that symbolizes the betrayal of an entire generation by the men who were officially their leaders. Although the first crime to be explored in *The Telling of Lies* is the death of Calder Maddox, the symbolic rape of Michael Riches's mind and body (repeated in the kidnap and brainwashing of Lily Porter) emerges as this novel's true "crime." As in *The Wars,* this crime involves the betrayal of trust by institutions whose mandate is to heal and protect, not to destroy, their fellow citizens.

But in *Lies,* other crimes and other pasts further complicate this pattern of finding a larger, unacknowledged crime behind the apparent crime of the present. The story of Vanessa's internment in the Japanese concentration camp during the Second World War emerges gradually and in pieces, beginning with her dedication of her diary to "Colonel Norimitsu—who, with one hand, killed my father and with the other made of my father's grave a garden" (*Lies,* 8). In a familiar pattern to Findley readers, the colonel combines violence and beauty in ways that problematize the identification of monstrosity. When two of his men are forced to kill themselves as punishment for attempting to rape a woman, he tells Vanessa, as if to explain his actions: "*No one is totally monstrous; not even monsters*" (15). Vanessa does not learn the truth of this statement until the end of the novel, when she is forced to recognize her own affinity with those whom she would oppose. Just as it is love that leads Hooker and Robert into killing, so it is her love for Meg Riches that forces Vanessa to acknowledge her own capacity for killing.

Vanessa's process of detection becomes an act of partial self-discovery as she relives her memories of the camp and of her relationships at the hotel with her three childhood friends: Lily Porter, who has become Calder Maddox's mistress and who has given Vanessa the diary as an early birthday present; Mercedes Mannheim, who helps Vanessa solve the mystery; and the Canadian, Marguerite Riches, called Meg, who, Vanessa eventually learns, has committed the murder. Vanessa's adoration of Meg, her own most private memories, and her strong desire to forget some of the memories seared on her psyche from her time in the prison camp at Bandung further complicate her ability to understand the plot she gradually uncovers.

Calder Maddox's murder on the beach is the second murder Vanessa has witnessed. In the camp, she saw her father killed as he tried to make his way from the men's camp to the women's to see his wife and daughter. Her father was executed by the enemy for disobeying rules during a war. Many, including Vanessa's fellow inmates, saw this context as providing a justification for his killing. For Vanessa, nothing can justify this death, although she refrains from blaming the man who ordered it or the culture within whose rules he was operating. In the course of the novel, she returns obsessively to the parallels between the two deaths and the emotions that this repetition of the most traumatic event of her life is forcing her to remember.

She and her mother witnessed her father's death but were prevented from going to him. Her mother, unable to cope with the brutality of the truth, suppresses it, choosing to remember instead a fiction of her husband dying in her arms. Vanessa, forced to participate in this revised memory, is never allowed an opportunity to come to terms with her own starker memories of his death. Her mother's death the year before the novel opens frees her to remember the past in her own way, but it is Maddox's death that initiates the process.

During Calder Maddox's murder, Vanessa is present and taking photographs but misses the significance of what she sees. It is only in retrospect that she learns that she has witnessed a murder. In seeking Maddox's murderer, she seems to be trying to compensate for the helplessness she felt witnessing the earlier murder by taking decisive action now. What she learns, however, is that a final judgment and subsequent action is no more possible in this case than in the other. When she learns that her best friend, Meg, has killed Maddox in revenge for the destruction of Meg's husband Michael's life through the brainwashing experiments enabled by Maddox's drugs, Vanessa's loyalty is entirely with Meg, but paradoxically the alliance with Meg forces her into an alliance with Meg's enemies. Vanessa thus becomes a very complicated kind of collaborator, complicit with forces she opposes yet unable to act otherwise. In a sense, this replicates her emotional sense of collaboration with Colonel Norimitsu during the war. Because he recognizes her mourning for her father's death when her mother does not, they develop an unspoken sense of affinity as each tries to read the mystery of the other. When he returns her mother's wedding ring, she is complicit in understanding that she must appear to be punished for having traded it. Her punishment is the cover-up that hides his acknowledgment of their special relationship in his return of the ring.

Meg, on the other hand, like Hooker in *Crazy People* and Robert in *The Wars,* murders out of her complicated sense of duty and love, which the novel respects but does not grant full endorsement, in my view. For her, the murder is largely a symbolic gesture, like Robert's freeing of the horses: a statement that she rejects Maddox's view of the world and his power. She reasserts control of her own life, refusing to be a victim by casting herself as the agent of death who paradoxically kills to affirm the sanctity of human life. This is a futile and misguided gesture, a result of Meg's complete isolation from other human beings for several years. It is also, perhaps, a commentary on how Vanessa, Meg's only friend according to Baby Frazier, has failed her through refusing to become a confidante.

Vanessa is one of Findley's most complex and interesting characters. Like his other central characters, she is defined by the quality of her witness and how she acts as a result, but unlike other characters, she is not an innocent observer nor is she a broken dreamer. Meg and her husband Michael are the broken dreamers of this text. Like Ruth of *Plague,* Meg has the athletic body of a swimmer, but like Robert of *The Wars,* she is more committed to conquering space than time. Vanessa says of her: "*Further—not faster* might have been her motto." Vanessa notes that there is a sense of something "always being withheld," a quality of "*something unsafe*" about Meg, giving her "a contradictory aura of intense tranquillity" (144). Michael, like *The Wars'* Robert, "had been so beautiful, once" but now he is "scarred; he is wounded" (33); he is "a shell" (32). At the beginning of the novel, Vanessa says of his destruction: "It is not my business" (33). The penetration of the mystery shows her that she is wrong. It both is and should be her business, because on the personal level, Michael is the husband of her best friend, and on the public level, Michael has been destroyed by the unholy alliance of drug companies and doctors symbolized by the partnership of Maddox and Dr. Chilcott. As Vanessa notes of these two men: "One made drugs—the other pushed them" (179). Vanessa is complicit in their empire. She relies on drugs to maintain her own precarious health and she has accepted the authority of those prescribing these drugs without question. Lawrence, her niece's husband and her companion in detection, has a different view of medical practice that rejects drugs for slower but ultimately more effective modes of treatment. His view leads to a less lucrative medical practice than Chilcott's and Vanessa has not considered its merits.

Although Vanessa resists introspection, her diary entries reveal as much about her character as they do of what she observes. Vanessa is 59 years old, a professional photographer and landscape gardener, and a listener, someone whose " 'elected silence' attracts the attention of gabblers and gossips" (18). She has deliberately created only "images of order and peace" in her garden designs and recorded only images of "[w]hat *is*" (27) in her photographs.

Vanessa has constructed herself in the image of Colonel Norimitsu, self-contained, disciplined, and "impossible to read" (201), in reaction to the revelation of her mother as "a reflection stranded in an abandoned mirror" (192) after her father's death. She told herself then that she was an orphan and vowed that she would never allow herself "to be defined as someone's widow or as someone's mother but only—forever—as my *self*" (130). Her mother had been oblivious to Vanessa's vigil for her dead father, but Colonel Norimitsu had watched and understood, making Vanessa feel that "[h]e knew. My vigil in the rain had meaning after all" (131). She knows that she testifies according to her witness, but Calder's death also reminds her that "[t]o be a witness is to be accountable" and she does not want to know that (132). She confesses her frustration with "[a]ll this ambivalence—all this wanting to know and not to know—to be and not to be accountable" (191). Her stability is fragile, hard-won, and difficult to maintain. She finds it difficult to confess, even to her diary, that she harbors rage: "I guess what I really didn't want to admit was that I hated Calder Maddox. Even now, as I write that down, I want to cross it out" (177). She also dislikes Lily Porter, not just for snobbish reasons of class prejudice, as Anne Bailey suggests in "Misrepresentations of Vanessa Van Horne: Intertextual Clues in *The Telling of Lies*,"[4] but because Lily reminds Vanessa of her own vulnerability as a girl and of her mother's loss of self in the love of her husband. Lily represents the chaos, confusion, and vulnerability that Vanessa most fears in herself. In contrasting photographs of herself at the hotel as a young girl right after Bandung and as a woman a year ago, Vanessa concludes with pride, "The person in the second photograph had definitely survived the person in the first. And yet, the person in the first had not had to die in order to guarantee that survival. Both are still with me; intact" (41). The older self protects the younger, but must also fear her impulses.

The hotel setting in this novel functions like the ark in *Voyage:* it provides an enclosed space in which an allegorical drama may unfold at a time of special pressure, when the social contracts that invisibly enable people to function are made visible. Vanessa thinks: "This place has become, in its way, a little like Bandung. . . . Calder's death has become a wire around this beach—a fence around our behaviour" (190). She is careful to distinguish between the ways in which the internment camp and the hotel are different. They are in no way directly comparable. Yet she is interested in the way such situations of extremity bring out similar human reactions. She writes: "No. This is not the same. But the blindness is. And its willfulness" (104). She sees these traits in others; the reader must learn to see them in Vanessa's narrative as well.

She sees the hotel as a symbol of the past and of a lost way of life where social divisions were regularly policed to enforce a conformity and elitism that was very comfortable for those who were secure at the top, as her family was. The book is dedicated to the Atlantic House Hotel, where Findley's own family enjoyed a similar tradition. In the novel, the Aurora Sands Hotel serves the double function of symbolizing a past that is being willfully destroyed while in its final days providing the setting for a larger drama that reveals citizens who fail to do their duty by allowing their attention to their civic responsibilities to lapse.

Vanessa had thought the hotel was a space of safety to oppose eternally to the vulnerabilities of Bandung, but what she discovers through investigating the murder is that "*{s}o—all our memories are wrong. The violence has been here always*" (158). The myth of a North American innocence has been exploded. The intertextual references to Thomas Mann's novel *Death in Venice* reinforce this realization. Vanessa notes that her niece, Petra, "is reading *Death in Venice*. This is almost too alarmingly appropriate" (106). Her invocation of Mann's image of beach vacationers "watching for signs of the plague" (106) suggests that the iceberg, like the monarch butterflies in *Plague,* is the sign of a disaster that flaws in the civilization have brought upon itself. Aschenbach's self-destructive desire for the beauty of the boy in *Death in Venice* suggests possible parallels in Findley's text: the tyranny of Vanessa's desire for order and her blinding infatuation with Meg that prevents her seeing for most of the story that Meg is the murderer she seeks; or Calder Maddox as the analogue for Aschenbach, the man whose passion for chemical experiments leads to his death by the devices he has invented.

Maddox's death has been preceded by another mystery: the arrival of an iceberg during the middle of summer on the coast of Maine, visible from the hotel's beach the morning of the murder. Like the butterflies in *Plague,* the iceberg is a multivalent symbol. It is the mystery that both attracts and defies explanation. Nine-tenths submerged, it represents the privacy and mystery of Vanessa's psyche, even to herself. Although some think it looks like the Capitol building in Washington, and eventually the murder can be traced back to the Capitol by a convoluted route Vanessa follows in seeking responsibility, such a reading of its meaning is clearly spurious, a result of a desire to make the meaningless meaningful rather than a rational clue. The scientists call the iceberg a *"stabilized renegade"* (133). Such a description invites an allegorical reading, but it is not easy to decide which characters the novel is presenting in such terms. Clearly Meg and Vanessa could be seen as stabilized renegades, but so could their enemies: the doctors and government agents who manufacture the cover-up. Each group is a renegade from the perspective of the other group. The stalemate reached at the end of the novel means that everyone's renegade behavior is stabilized for the moment at least.

Is renegade behavior to be admired or deplored? The novel reminds us that society functions according to an unwritten contract in which everyone agrees to obey the rules to prevent anarchy. When one group chooses to ignore the rules, their renegade behavior (the medical torture and destruction of Michael) seems to authorize further renegade behavior on the part of those who protest (Meg's murder of Maddox). Vanessa decides that she is prepared to move against her friend Lily, if necessary, to preserve Meg's secret. Most interpretations of the novel downplay this decision, given that it hardly seems necessary in the context of the novel where the authorities already know that Meg did it and have chosen not only to ignore this knowledge to protect their own affairs from scrutiny but actively to silence Lily themselves. My argument is that Vanessa's decision is not necessary to protect Meg, but it is necessary to enable Vanessa to save face. She was not there when Meg needed her before; she vows that she will be there next time.

Vanessa's sense of grievance is strong. She ends the novel with the lament that the sense of possibility with which she and her three friends began their lives has been betrayed. For her, the "rise and fall" of the hotel where they began their friendship and where the novel's action is situated "have been our rise and fall" (359). The hotel where she has spent every summer of her life except for the five spent in a Japanese internment camp during the war has been sold to developers and will be razed to prepare the way for a condominium. Vanessa feels rage, sorrow, and betrayal. Her sense of loss makes her feel both "dispossessed" and "impotent." She concludes: "Something I wanted to save has been destroyed behind my back" (1). By the end of the novel, she realizes much more clearly the extent of what has been destroyed; it is not just a hotel and a way of life but the trust and truth telling on which democracy depends.

Anne Bailey argues that the extent of Vanessa's unreliability as a narrator has been underestimated by critics, who confuse the position of the author of the novel with that of its narrator. In her view, this is "a sinister and pessimistic book" (Bailey, "Misrepresentations," 191). According to Bailey Vanessa's elitism leads her to value the Riches's lives above that of Lily Porter, the social upstart, but the reader should be wary of endorsing Vanessa's willingness to sacrifice Lily for them. Bailey suggests that the composition of Vanessa's diary deliberately misleads the reader, concentrating on the "red herring" of the police roadblocks when they have nothing to do with Maddox's murder. While I find Bailey's attention to the complexity of Vanessa's narration and motivation salutory, I think her obsession with murder and its punishment leads her to underestimate the thematic links between the various elements of the novel, none of which make sense as plotting devices nor seem meant to. What connects the iceberg, the murder, and the roadblocks? Vanessa's narrative desire and psychological need to assign blame so that she can ignore her own complicity. Bailey sees it as pernicious that Vanessa presents herself as a witness when in fact she is in control of the telling and shaping of her tale. Bailey seems to be asking, who really gets away with murder in this novel? In Bailey's view, Vanessa wants us to think it is the government to distract us from the fact that Meg goes unpunished for her action. But I think the novel makes the impossibility of innocence and the inevitability of complicity its central subject. The murder is the vehicle that sets the story in play but it is not the important story, to either Vanessa or the government, although for different reasons. Bailey seems to think that generically and morally the murder should be the focus of the story, but I think the effect of the book as a whole is to argue that it cannot be. The novel is labeled a mystery and not a detective story to mobilize ambiguity rather than destroy it. I read Maddox's murder as a sign to readers to pay attention to the murder of memory itself, to the rewriting of history that erases some stories to privilege others as well as to abuses of authority of various kinds that diminish the public's collective ability to know what is happening and to register dissent if dissent seems appropriate.

Critics such as Irvine, Pennee, and York, who see Vanessa coming to a positive resolution at the end of this text, focus less on the decision to protect Meg and more on the distinction that Vanessa's mother's friend, Arabella Barrie, makes between true justice and *"the Law as she is writ"* (*Lies,* 355). Arabella and Vanessa believe that the law must be interpreted contextually rather than absolutely. In expressing such a belief, they align themselves with what feminist Carole Gilligan identifies in her book *In a Different Voice* as a view of justice that is particular to women: A view that refuses final judgment until a full contextualization of the situation and its options is provided.[5]

In resisting the view that sees this decision as feminist, Anne Bailey raises two questions about this novel that she believes critics have failed to address: "[H]ow can murder in one case be heinous and in another politically redemptive? And, on a more specific level, why are Michael and Meg Riches's lives more valuable than Lily Porter's in Vanessa's view?" (Bailey, "Misrepresentation," 191). The first question is one I see Findley raising in all of his work because he sees it as both true and troubling that the prohibition against murder cannot or does not function absolutely. Although Bailey has phrased it as a rhetorical question, implying an absolute answer, I believe that this is a genuine question the novel wishes to raise for deep consideration. The second question follows from accepting the premise of the first: If it is argued that killing is allowable under certain circumstances, how can those circumstances be determined without the possibility of error or the abuse of power leading to further injustices? Findley suggests the troubling conclusion that people never can be absolutely sure that their decisions are correct but that they must continue to do their best by always paying attention. I agree with Bailey that the novel does not share Vanessa's implied decision that Lily Porter's life is less valuable than Meg's. The murder of Calder Maddox has solved nothing. It has not even served to publicize the evil he has done. Further deaths would be equally fruitless. What is needed is a level of public vigilance that can catch problems before they reach a dimension where murder seems the only recourse.

Unlike Bailey, I see the ending as positive because, for the first time, Vanessa accepts responsibility for the present state of affairs. She admits that she has failed to pay attention and vows that she will no longer ignore the wake-up call that the iceberg symbolizes for her. The green of Maddox's dead body and the bottom half of the iceberg is mirrored in the green of the shade Vanessa pulls to close the novel. Green is the color that calls citizens to their duty, imploring them to pay attention, and green is the color of hope, implying that if they heed the call, there is still a chance to create a better world than that envisioned by those for whom human lives have no inherent value.

Conjuring the Past

The value of individual lives and the civilizational plague that threatens them activate the multiple complex plots of Findley's next novel, *Headhunter*. If the focus of *Lies* is on the dangers of hiding, ignoring, and destroying the past, the focus of *Headhunter* falls on the ways in which people are doomed to repeat the past if its lessons are not learned. In this novel, Nicholas Fagan, the Irish writer Findley has invented as an alter ego and whose work is cited in *The Wars*, appears for the first time as a character and mentor to the novel's chief witness, Lilah Kemp, for whom "Fagan's voice was the voice of English literature itself" (*Headhunter*, 28). Fagan writes: "If I were to propose a text for the twentieth century, it would be Joseph Conrad's *Heart of Darkness*. As subtext, I would nominate Mary Shelley's *Frankenstein*. Nothing better illustrates than these two books the consequence of human ambition. On reading them again, I . . . took up my current view that the human race has found its destiny in self-destruction" (98). *Headhunter* may be read as a testing of this conclusion through recycling and recontextualizing the major characters and obsessions of these two canonical texts in a contemporary Canadian setting. Although the novel is supposedly set in the near future, the Toronto setting invoked is inspired by the 1980s.

Throughout this study I have argued that Findley regularly relocates a symbolic heart of darkness in paradoxical settings that often claim a monopoly on the light of civilization: in Hollywood in *Plague*, in Europe in *The Wars*, in the educated elite in *Words*, in God's heaven and Noah's regime in *Voyage*, and in the hotels of the rich on the seacoast of Maine in *Lies*. In *Headhunter*, drawing on imagery and characters first introduced in the title story of his short story collection *Dinner along the Amazon*, Findley explicitly invokes *Heart of Darkness* as the initiating intertext of a novel that systematically addresses yet again the vexed question of how civilization and barbarism are interconnected. To explore this theme he once again draws upon the close identification between the monster and his creator, most memorably dramatized in Shelley's *Frankenstein*. Kurtz and Frankenstein each symbolize the hubris of untrammeled ambition and the abuse of authority that accompanies it. The note preceding the text of *Headhunter* explains that "[i]n part, this novel tells the story of what could happen if the wrong people wielded authority" in Toronto's great psychiatric institutions. But just as Kurtz's monstrosity is balanced by Marlow's levelheaded dedication to duty, and Frankenstein's abandoning of his responsibility for the creation of his creature is balanced by the insistence of that creature that he assume responsibility, so each of these characters in Findley's remobilizing of their stories is centered through the erratic and powerful consciousness of Lilah Kemp.

The brilliance of this novel lies in its creation of the character of Lilah. She brings an eccentric, female perspective to these stories of male ambition and destruction. Her father was abusive and her loving mother was murdered by a stranger in a Toronto ravine with no one attending to her cries for help. By making Lilah a schizophrenic medium with the power to raise the dead, Findley transforms the metaphorical power of the imagination into the literal power to call forth life. Lilah can be seen as a figure for the artist and for the reader, and for the artist as reader. A retired librarian and an obsessive reader, Lilah provides a frame for the novel through her reading, which is the act that begins and ends the text.

Headhunter opens with another of Findley's shockingly inventive beginnings. When Lilah inadvertently releases Kurtz from page 92 of Conrad's *Heart of Darkness,* she sets a new narrative in motion, that of Findley's *Headhunter.* What sets Kurtz free? Is it an act of inattention on Lilah's part as she sits "lulled by words and water" (4), or an act of such profound attention to the text that she forgets momentarily to attend to her own power in losing herself to that of the text? Lilah's "intense but undisciplined powers" (3) point to a paradox at the heart of Findley's constant injunction to readers to "pay attention." In attending so closely to the text, Lilah brings it into being in her own space and time, losing control of the characters once she has brought them into existence.

The omniscient narrator of the opening scene presents this dilemma playfully, despite the horror of many of the beings that Lilah has accidentally conjured. The parody of Conrad is overt. Kurtz's escape takes place in the heart of the library, the institutional repository of the images and ideas that have shaped the contemporary world, beside the artificial greenery that frames a man-made pool. Conrad's jungle in the heart of

Africa has been transposed into the library in the heart of Canada's financial capital, Toronto. The library is constituted by a will to classify, codify, and collect knowledge that has come to define the essence of Western civilization. Kurtz's materialization in this new space, with "the smell of old, dried paper . . . printer's ink and binding glue" still on him (4), suggests that the library is the jungle from which *Headhunter*'s heart of darkness is appropriately unleashed.

Lilah's release of Kurtz shows that there is a cost to the reader's imaginative immersion in the world of others through reading books. Sympathetic identification can lead to annihilation. Lilah's mother, Sarah (herself a medium), is murdered when she mistakenly conjures Mister Hyde (from Robert Louis Stevenson's *Doctor Jekyll and Mister Hyde*). Several years before the action of this novel begins, Lilah has conjured a Nazi book-burner named Otto who burns the Rosedale Public Library, which she loved and where she had happily worked as chief librarian. Her responsibility for the burning of the books reveals her own complicity in the horror she dreads from Kurtz. Their conflict is not posed in the simplistic oppositions of "us" versus "them" but rather through the tangled emotions of a character so involved in humanity that her rejection of Kurtz comes from intimate knowledge of the harm he can do rather than any assumption of moral superiority.

When, at the end of the book, Kurtz is safely returned to the ending that Conrad wrote for him, Lilah returns to her present, moved by the story she has read and relived in its transformed rewriting, and relieved that Kurtz has been returned to his proper place between the pages of a book. The ending of *Headhunter* challenges its readers to move beyond the frame, connecting the text they have just read back to the world in which they live. Lilah's perspective on events is endorsed by the omniscient narration to such an extent that readers willingly suspend disbelief to accept the central fiction that Kurtz has indeed materialized to live out his horror in the heart of Toronto. When Lilah sits on her bed with *Heart of Darkness* beside her and thinks back on *Headhunter*'s story, she wonders: "*Who would believe it?*" . . . *It's only a book,* they would say. *That's all it is. A story. Just a story*" (440). This imagined dismissal of the validity of the story that readers have just experienced invites rebuttal. Lilah believes that stories can be true. Findley's readers are encouraged to share this faith. Those who would dismiss Lilah's reading of reality have already been discredited in the course of the narrative. They are the psychiatric establishment who prescribe her drugs to suppress her special gifts, blurring her ability to see clearly but enabling her to cope with the world on their terms. "Murder by milligrams" is the narrator's description for their cure. Lilah hates her doctor for depriving her of "her world of wonders" and trying to "take away her powers" (30). To deal with Kurtz, she suspends taking her medication, but when he has been exposed and dispatched from her story, she resumes the medication.

Findley told Jeffrey Canton: "I believe that madness and the imagination walk a fine line."[6] Lilah's schizophrenia walks that line, leading to both blindness and insight. Margaret Atwood suggests in the afterword to *The Journals of Susanna Moodie* that all Canadians must live with a metaphorical collective schizophrenia, as immigrants to the North American place.[7] For her, schizophrenia is a metaphor for the dis-ease and inventiveness of invader-settler colonialism. Fagan's comments on Canada echo Atwood's analysis (*Headhunter*, 258). *Headhunter* absorbs Atwood's usage into its own deployment of schizophrenia as a multivalent metaphor. At a personal level, it is a sign for the glories and vulnerabilities of the human imagination; at a textual level, it operates as the sign enabling intertextuality as "a mosaic of quotations"; at a political level, it suggests the ongoing dialogue between past and present.[8]

The artist, Slade, whose "brightly coloured harlequin jacket" marks his function as the Harlequin or Conradian disciple to Kurtz (*Headhunter*, 66), also walks the schizophrenic line. He wants to dedicate his violent paintings to Kurtz, "*the man who released my demons*" (60). Slade's statement about his paintings "*The Collection of the Golden Chambers*" reads: "*You will see here . . . savage acts which have been done too long in darkness. It is my belief they should be done in the light. And to that end—these paintings*" (67). They are in part the visual equivalent of the novel itself in that they make visible the nightmare of forbidden desires, of surrender to consumption, of manipulation, degradation, and torture offered up to a "casual horror" (70). The novel, however, argues that such acts should not happen at all, in darkness or in light, and it locates resistance to the practice of such acts largely in its female characters, in the ghosts from the past, and in the voice of the unborn child in Olivia Wylie's womb, all of whom echo the refrain "[s]ave the children." The paintings show no women, only "males in thrall of being male" (68), as if to confirm Griffin Price's judgment on the Toronto elite as "*a social class of rogues and brutes dressed up in pinstripe suits and screwing everything in sight*" (62). This judgment is part of a longer passage linking Canada's colonial heritage, its rapacious capitalist present, and the limited roles prescribed for men in such a system. Fagan later echoes this analysis in his account of his journey upriver into the heart of the continent as a journey into the horror of environmental and cultural destruction: "This that was once a living place for humankind has become their killing ground" (259).

Slade's most horrific painting, *"The Golden Chamber of the White Dogs,"* repeats the signature Conradian image of horror, staked human heads, within the setting of a modern operating room depicted as a scene of sexual torture. What Kurtz finds most unnerving yet mesmerizing about the painting is that "each and every figure was rampant with sexual menace and power—even those who were displayed as victims" (68). Victim and victimizer alike are portrayed as "willing addicts of desire" (426). What the novel shows is that this apparent willingness is manufactured through the administration of drugs and sleep deprivation and, even so, is violently resisted by its victims. The painting acts as a litmus test for revealing the character of each of its viewers. Emma, forced to take a second look at the painting by her husband's insistence that horror is how he makes his living, finds nothing of interest except for the dogs, which remind her of the prowling fears that invade her dreams. Later, when it is hanging in the foyer of the institute, Lilah sees it as the sign of Kurtz's power over his domain and a warning to her to act to stop him, and the Wylie women see it as an inappropriate image of hell to hang in what should be an asylum for hope.

At the art show opening, the businessman Shapiro drunkenly confesses to Kurtz his arousal, self-recognition, and frustration at the inhibitions that prevent him from admitting his own murderous, pedophilic, and incestuous desires. Shapiro seems to interpret the painting, with Kurtz's assent, as granting him the permission to move out of control, into the rape and murder of his son George: the novel's ultimate horror. Kurtz, like Shapiro, sees in the figures' "inflammatory nakedness" an invitation to join in the beauty and power of madness (71) and immediately sets out to buy the painting for the foyer of his institute. He buys the painting with money (designated for research) donated by the businessman Gordon Perry in gratitude for Kurtz's central role in delivering to him both the boy, Warren Ellis, and the family fortune he desired. In these ways the painting links the Conradian version of headhunters to their contemporary incarnations as businessmen and psychiatrists and to a male appetite for power that is devouring the world.

The novel's opening section ends with Lilah watching Kurtz walk out of the library into the street. She thinks: "Kurtz, the harbinger of darkness. Kurtz, the horror-meister. Kurtz, the headhunter" (6). "Headhunter" is a pivotal term in the translation of *Heart of Darkness* from the context of late nineteenth-century contestations of colonialism into late twentieth-century investigations of that legacy in the contemporary faces of neocolonialism. In the invader-settler context of Canada, fictional representations of the colonial encounter have usually involved settler attempts to appropriate the native, as Conrad does the African, to a European agenda. But in *Headhunter*, the focus falls on the interrogation of the settler psyche, shifting the primary reference of the word "headhunter" from the myth of the savage who literally collects human heads (providing the imperialist justification for the "civilizing mission") to contemporary psychiatrists working within the health care system to manage mental illness, and to twentieth-century capitalists recruiting corporate raiders. What links the psychiatrists and the capitalists in Findley's novel is the shared obsession with power and the violence it engenders. Even the plastic surgeon, James Berry, aspires, like Kurtz, to the role of God. Conrad's Kurtz is a successful ivory trader and an experimenter in the limits of human debauchery. Findley's Kurtz trades in information control over the lives of the rich and powerful, information he translates into the cash to fund experimental research on human bodies, minds, and souls, which he treats as commodities. His official title is Psychiatrist-in-Chief at the Parkin Institute of Psychiatric Research. Just as the idealistic memo of Conrad's Kurtz includes its coda to "[e]xterminate the brutes," so Findley's Kurtz produces a memo documenting his search for *"absolute power"* via the motto *"psychiatry is my mode, psychiatric research is my delivery system . . . Under my guidance, they will soon enough become the willing addicts of desire"* (426).

This is a resonant image for the kind of "psychic driving" critiqued in *Lies*. It has parallels in the image of zombification for the colonial usurpation of the bodies and minds of the colonized in Caribbean writer Erna Brodber's novel *Myal*. Whereas the mind control of *Lies* manipulates memory and knowledge, Kurtz's ambition extends to the full range of human desire, including the sexual. Peggy Wylie's initial misreading of the sign "Therapist" to read "The rapist" reveals her intuitive understanding of Kurtz's true agenda (322). In this novel, there are two groups of rapists: the psychiatrists who share in Kurtz's ambition, especially Dr. Shelley, and the members of the Club of Men, the corporate establishment, whom Kurtz controls through pandering to their desires.

Cannibalism is the unspoken ultimate horror in Conrad's text. *Headhunter* returns the concept from its assignment to racial others back to the West responsible for this initial projection onto others, but in the process links the idea of cannibalism to another potent Western taboo, that of incest. *Headhunter* changes the scene of cannibalistic incest from the literal eating of the bodies of others to the fathers' metaphorical devouring of their children, body and soul, through the acts of sexual rape and murder. The unpunished rape and murder of George Shapiro by his father and fellow members of the Club of Men *"out of control"* (421) is documented through words and photographs in the files of the institute. For Kurtz, who is described as "a voyeur of voyeurism" (146), the children and their parents are experimental subjects revealing the capacities of a new drug to produce docility and compliance in its victims, and enabling Kurtz to exploit the crossed desires of children and fathers alike.

Although Lilah initially believes that she has been chosen to be Kurtz's Marlow (27), a Dr. Charles Marlow, another psychiatrist, arrives to share this function with her shortly after Kurtz's appearance in the library. Lilah works in partnership with Marlow, removing the stolen files of Kurtz's victims from the institute after the suicide of Dr. Purvis and ensuring that Marlow discovers the evidence in them that he needs to convince him of Kurtz's wrongdoing. Marlow fails to attend to Dr. Purvis's anguish. Unable to confront Kurtz or confide in Marlow, Purvis takes his own life. Marlow also ignores Lilah's cryptic warnings and the attempted interventions of Dr. Eleanor Farjeon, who tries to save the human detritus from these experiments, children who seem to be "refugees from nightmares" (158). Her death by decapitation appears to have been engineered by Kurtz, perhaps through another doctor's work on mind control and thought transference, to prevent her speaking of her theories explaining the children's problems and tracing them back to Kurtz.

The discovery of George's rape and murder in the files and the arrival of Kurtz's lost manifesto through the agency of helpful secretaries finally prompt Marlow to act, but Lilah has already conjured Kurtz's death from Conrad's novel: *"The wilderness had found him out, and had taken upon him a terrible vengeance . . ."* (406). When Marlow arrives to confront Kurtz with the evidence he has discovered, he finds that Kurtz has already succumbed to the plague. Like *The Butterfly Plague* and *The Telling of Lies*, *Headhunter* uses imagery of plague to characterize the self-destructiveness of a civilization gone mad in its quest for power. In *Headhunter*, the plague is called sturnusemia. Birds and other animals are blamed for its transmission but it is revealed that they are merely the designated scapegoats for a disease that has its true cause in government experiments gone wrong. The whistle-blowing civil servant, Smith Jones, an immunologist who sought to reveal the truth, has been silenced through the agency of Kurtz, who has had him committed to an asylum for the criminally insane. His truth telling was labeled lies. It seems poetic justice that Kurtz should fall victim to this plague unleashed by the same experimental forces to which he has surrendered himself. The disease reveals itself through a speckling of the skin, a "speckulation" that, in its echo of financial speculation, further reinforces the links between the uncontrolled ambition that unleashes the plague, the uncontrolled experiments of Kurtz with human lives, and the driving desires of capitalism as a system that puts money and power above the sanctity of life. Marlow thinks of the sound links suggested by the word "speckulation": "*specktator—specktacle—specktacular. And specktral*" (386). These words encapsulate the action of the novel, revealing the links between voyeurism, the substitution of image for substance, and death. Because Kurtz specializes in "the foibles of the rich" (49), he has become a voyeur/witness to all the corruptions that money can buy, including the deaths of the innocent.

Surrounded by his "famous ivory collection," Kurtz has "the look of a priest gone native in a nineteenth-century outpost of empire" (430). His god is himself and his sin is hubris. He explains that he had no interest in the rapes or murder in themselves: "The activity itself was puerile. My only interest lay in bringing two desiring factions together. I melded them. I made them one" (431). In creating this monster he has made himself into a monster, like Dr. Frankenstein before him. Echoing Conrad's Kurtz, he explains: "I had immense plans. I was on the threshold of great things . . ." (433). Like Findley's other megalomaniacs, Kurtz believes in his vision. Marlow learns that "[h]e believed in ashes. He believed in burning down minds and memories—turning them into ash. *Out of ashes—miracles,* he said" (434).

When Marlow looks for an explanation, Kurtz confesses that he wanted to be his own father (435). Here indeed is the banality of evil that Hannah Arendt found at the heart of the Nazi horror. Fabiana Holbach, Kurtz's "Intended," echoes this explanation: "He wanted to please his father—not himself. He wanted to fulfil his father's dream—not his own" (437). She loved and remembered a man caught up in "the adventure of science" but tormented by this need to please an implacable and mocking father. This explanation seems radically insufficient if taken at face value in the context of the horrors of this novel, yet surely that is the novel's point. There can be no adequate explanation for such callousness. In the context of Findley's work as a whole, Kurtz's explanation fits the pattern of linking familial and public worlds through an attention to abdications of responsibility at every level, from that of the parent to that of the agents of the state, all metaphorically named "the fathers" in Findley's fictional world.

Findley's Marlow lies to Fabiana, his Kurtz's Intended, just as Conrad's Marlow lied to the Intended of Conrad's Kurtz. He thinks, *"{W}e write each other's lives—by means of fictions. Sustaining fictions. Uplifting fictions. Lies"* (438). Like Vanessa at the end of *Lies,* he rejects absolute values in favor of what seems most needed to sustain survival at a given moment. He leaves Fabiana the comfort of her illusions, but he is on his way to confront Dr. Shelley and the guilty members of the Club of Men with the truth. Earlier, Olivia Wylie's cynical thoughts on lying provide a context for understanding Marlow's actions here. She thinks: "In the past, you were lied to *for your own good.* Now, you were lied to for the good of others" (13). Is Marlow lying for Fabiana or for himself? His lying makes him complicit with the forces he opposes, something he recognizes when he lies to Amy Wylie, the schizophrenic poet. Amy and Lilah never lie. Their inability to lie is a symptom of their disease. In their society, this is an affliction to be cured. Amy's madness is described as "benevolence" (370), but it could also be described as the ability to imagine otherwise. Lilah shares this affliction. If Lilah had been capable of fully taking on Marlow's role and redeeming the world from Kurtz on her own, then perhaps the ending would have been different. As the story stands, the novel shows Canadian society repeating the hypocrisies that Conrad castigates in turn-of-the-century imperial Belgium.

Nicholas Fagan summarizes Marlow's function in a letter to Lilah that she reads on the last page of the book. According to Fagan, "Every Kurtz must have his Marlow—and Marlow will always come to take Kurtz home." Fagan wonders why Marlow would agree to such a role and speculates that "it is because he is beholden to Kurtz for having provided him, after darkness, with a way to find new light" (440). This reasoning suggests that each new generation in each invented community must reenter its own particular heart of darkness in search of its own Kurtz—its own destructive desires. Violence and beauty, good and evil, are inseparably intertwined. Books are the guide on that journey to this knowledge. They lead from the darkness of horror to the light of compassion. Although Kurtz seems oblivious to the literary reference of his name in conjunction with Marlow's, Marlow not only sees the coincidence but regularly uses literature for psychotherapy. But in showing the darkness truthfully, literature must recreate its erotic attraction as well as its viciousness, risking charges of voyeurism or pornography. In taking these risks, *Headhunter* does not question these culturally loaded terms of darkness and light as a postcolonial theorist might. Instead, the novel continues to privilege literature and light, as the Western tradition it celebrates and interrogates always has.

Many critics think that *Headhunter* is too long, too loaded with intertextual references to most of the great books of English, American, and Canadian literature, and too undisciplined in the range of stories it seeks to tell. As a novel on the attractions and dangers of excess, it embodies excess in its own structure. I have stressed *Heart of Darkness* and *Frankenstein* as threads the reader can follow to make sense of the narrative sprawl, but these other stories do more than repeat the themes of Western civilization's self-destruction in other registers. They also suggest that their chaotic coexistence in Lilah's mind and the novel's world implies a change in how literary tradition is perceived. Instead of viewing the literary heritage of the past chronologically, Lilah and the novel view it spatially. Her mother describes her gift as the ability to cut *"through time"* (256). Although Lilah is trapped in her body with her unreliably schizophrenic mind, she can conjure characters out of any other time into her own. She experiences the literary tradition, as any eclectic reader may, as an immediate kaleidoscope of images rather than as a sequence that has grown and changed over time. These other characters and their plots are not influences on Findley's text; they are analogues he invokes to mark the continuities and differences that he sees between their worlds and his own.

Lilah's desires speak most strongly through her very personal relationship with four intertexts in particular: Emily Bronte's *Wuthering Heights,* the Anglo-Saxon epic *Beowulf,* Beatrix Potter's *Peter Rabbit,* and the nineteenth-century Canadian settler-writer Susanna Moodie. Lilah pushes a baby buggy with her wherever she goes. Inside the buggy lies *"Wuthering Heights—in blue"* (10). In her mind, the buggy transports her lost child, Linton, her child from her demon-rapist Heathcliff. Marlow's dog, Grendel, retrieves the female monster killed by Beowulf as a faithful companion fearful of his beheaded mother who calls to him from the darkness to which she has been exiled. Peter Rabbit's shoes are the talisman Lilah clutches, holding childhood innocence and truth telling up as a shield against the horrors of the world around her. Lilah rescued the curmudgeonly Susanna Moodie from the library fire and now they are friends. Moodie's courage and knowledge of what it means to lose one's children fortify Lilah's spirit in her own quest to save the children. These incarnations of characters and objects from other texts explain Lilah's character and are explicable through her schizophrenia.

The incarnations of Emma Bovary (from Flaubert's *Madame Bovary*) as Emma Berry and of Jay Gatsby (from Fitzgerald's *The Great Gatsby*) as James Gatz seem to provide external corroboration for the validity of Lilah's perspective on the world as being essentially more sane than that of the people who judge her insane because it is unclear whether or not these individuals can be attributed to Lilah's conjuring. Emma Bovary and Jay Gatsby are two of literature's most compelling figures for an addiction to desire, which Emma pursues through courting the danger of illicit sex and Jay through information control, money, and glamour. Findley's incarnations of these characters show them as fleeing unhappy pasts which eventually catch up to them and destroy them. Emma has deliberately named herself after Emma Bovary in an attempt to flee her Saskatchewan childhood and the sterility of her marriage. James ran away from his violent and incestuous father in childhood and has been in flight ever since. Together they construct a fantasy world that is destroyed on the verge of its consummation through the murderous return of Jay's father. This subplot thus repeats the novel's concern with learning the lessons of history and literature in another key.

But James and Emma's story also introduces the theme of the watching child and the judging servant first seen in *Crazy People,* in a further set of echoing scenes and stories. Barbara Berry, Emma's daughter, is another of Findley's precocious and neglected watchful children who considers herself an orphan (165). Barbara blames her father for her mother's malaise. A plastic surgeon, he had completely reconstructed Emma's face after a traffic accident, turning her into a great beauty. Barbara accuses him of wiping out who she really was when all he had to do was restore her. He turned her into "someone else," someone for him to look at (395). Barbara's words suggest that her father is another version of Kurtz, one that cannot be banished back into the pages of a book at the end of the story.

Barbara's conversations with the black servant Orley reveal further derogations of responsibility. When Orley and her husband, Bobby Hawkins, had called the police after their convenience store was robbed years earlier, the police came and shot Bobby "[b]ecause he was black— and he was there" (168). Orley, deciding to deny the world another victim, aborted her child and vowed never to release her rage. Now she regrets that decision. Her story reflects upon the dilemma of Olivia Wylie, who is trying to decide whether or not to abort her own recently conceived child. Olivia decides to give birth as an act of faith in the possibility of creating a better world. Each of these stories hammers home the theme of responsibilities betrayed and a civilization self-destructing through a failure to come to terms with its legacies from the past.

One of the files assigned to Marlow is that of Timothy Findley, the writer. Part of the Findley transcript claims that writers and psychiatrists *"do the same thing . . . We're both trying to find out what makes the human race tick. And the way we do that—both of us—is by climbing down inside other people's lives to see if they're telling the truth or not. Most of us are lying"* (142). *Headhunter* continues the inquiry into the "telling of lies" begun most openly in *Famous Last Words* and continued through *Voyage* and *Lies*. As in the earlier novels, the human will to be and the literary words that record human survival are, paradoxically, the antidote to lies. Fagan, the narrator explains, published stories but "had never written fiction. What he did was create an imagined setting for truths, where they could be seen in ways that life did not present them" (256). For example, he published a fable that invented a history that might have been: the assassination of Jean-Paul Sartre and Simone de Beauvoir. The story allegorically demonstrates the death of philosophy in *Headhunter*'s desolate world. The point of the fable is "the dangerous consequences of failing to pay attention—and the savage consequences of ignorance" (270). *Headhunter*'s method emulates Fagan's example. The world it depicts is the most savage Findley has imagined, yet in its complexity and power it is also one of his most successful achievements. To combat ignorance, Findley conjures multiple ghosts from Toronto's past and the entire Western literary tradition.

Chapter Six
Findley's Families

This chapter could have been called "More Crazy People." Readers who interpreted the title of Findley's first novel, *The Last of the Crazy People*, as a promise rather than a lament discovered that it initiated an extended inquiry into the question of madness, its social definition and its social role, rather than an obituary for the end of a theme. But there is an especially intimate connection between *The Last of the Crazy People* and *The Piano Man's Daughter*, for what is decisively ended in the first novel is resurrected and granted renewal in Findley's most recent full-length fiction: the impasse of the southern Ontario Tory tradition represented by the privileged families who had dominated cultural life in this small part of the British empire at the turn of the century. *The Piano Man's Daughter* and Findley's novella, *You Went Away*, retreat from the horrific futuristic vision of *Headhunter* back to the past that provided Lilah and her allies with the sustaining vision to fight the death dealers of their world.

The novel and the novella reveal the dark secrets beneath the facade of the nuclear family. In *The Piano Man's Daughter*, it is the secret of inherited mental illness and the shame of children born to single mothers; in *You Went Away*, it is the shame of a physically and emotionally absent father. Findley's play *The Stillborn Lover* continues probing the pain caused by the gap between the facade and the reality of family life. Many of Findley's short stories examine broken families of various kinds and experimental attempts at creating alternative family structures outside the model of the heterosexual nuclear family. Findley adopts the feminist slogan that the personal is political to insist there is an intimate relation between the devastating wars of the twentieth century and these multitudes of unhappy families. This is an intuitive rather than a fully reasoned analytical theme in his work. The strengths of these dramas lie in their emotional intensity, the eloquence of the pain they express, and their insistence in clinging to the vestiges of hope in the very element that constitutes humanity's greatest vulnerability: its mortality.

Asylums on Fire

The Piano Man's Daughter has close affinities with the story of Cassandra Wakelin from Findley's play *Can You See Me Yet?*, which is dedicated to his grandmother E. M. Fagan Bull. The early play and the late novel share plot and thematic similarities, focusing on the loneliness of an exceptional child within the family, the tyrannies of patriarchal dominance, and the charged symbolisms of the doubled meanings of asylum as both sanctuary and prison, and of fire as agent of both life and death. Canada as an isolated backwater of British Empire is shown to be no safer than anywhere else.

Set in an asylum for the insane in 1938, *Can You See Me Yet?* centers around the interplay between Cassandra's present life in the asylum and her memories of the past within her family, played against the backdrop of impending world war. The play's epigraph, from a poem by Margaret Atwood, introduces Findley's theme of a character living "on the edges." Cassandra is schizophrenic. She carries a photograph album with pictures of her family from her past and confuses the patients in the new wing she has entered with various members of her family. Of the album she says, "This book is all I have that tells me who I am."[1] Each patient, except Cassandra, plays a double role of both patient and family member as Cassandra conjures up scenes from the past from her photographs, interweaving past and present.

Unhappy in the asylum, Cassandra thinks she wants to return home, but when she does, in her imagination, she finds only misery. Her father owned a piano factory and they had money, but she felt she could never please him. After her mother died Cassandra left, hoping to become a missionary in China, but she couldn't do it, returning home a failure to find her family fortunes had fallen. She blames her father for treating his children like things, and preferring her older brother, Patrick, who died on the battlefields of the First World War, and her younger sister, Rosemary, who marries to retrieve the family fortunes. Her brother Franklin believes that his father has castrated him. He blames the father for his own impotence and for Patrick's death, and the father's generation for the death of all the children whose graves he saw on the battlefield graveyards of Europe (*Yet,* 157).

Cassandra's dream has been to achieve perfection, to make herself a god, and "[a] better god than is, not some blind maniac lost in the dark—but a god who could look down and see me where I stand" (162). She blames herself for her failure to save her disciple, or even a dog. In her "War Sermon," in the middle of the play, with the sound of Hitler's speech in the background over the radio, she cries, "[T]here's something eager and malignant in us all that yearns to cringe, wants to be obedient. That is the secret of their power. Our willing weakness" (121). Cassandra embodies both the uncompromising drive for perfection and the complicit abjection that in Findley's view enabled fascism's triumph as the ultimate expression of modernism's desire to create a new god in its own image. But as her name suggests, she is doomed to have her message unattended.

Only Doberman, the man who thinks he is a dog, responds to her kindness and saves her from suicide at the end of the play. His action initiates her acceptance among the other inmates. The final words of the play, however, are the nurse's announcement that "[i]n September of 1939, the Asylum at Britton was destroyed by fire. Cassandra Wakelin died. But her arms, in death, had gathered to her *others*, and she did not die alone. As she had lived" (166). This ending, like all of Findley's endings, gives as it takes away. Before she dies, the "dog" Doberman and the other inmates "see" her, giving her the reciprocal gaze she has craved; but the price of this recognition is a fiery death, not just for her but for all of them. The fire that consumes her is both her own longing for perfection and its mirror in the Nazi declaration of war and launching of the fires of holocaust and the reciprocal response in the bombs of nuclear annihilation dropped by the Allies on Japan. I have traced the variations on these themes and images throughout Findley's work, but they recur in a particularly concentrated form in *The Piano Man's Daughter*.

The Piano Man's Daughter is narrated by Charlie Kilworth, a 29-year-old piano tuner, who tells the story of his mother's life as a means of recording his own quest for his lost and unknown father, and thus for his own identity as a person. He describes this dilemma quaintly to his mother's girlhood friend Eleanor: "[T]he authorship of my life seem[s] to have been misplaced."[2] His search for origins becomes his way of creating himself. The novel therefore takes the form of an elegiac romance, in which the narrator, supposedly telling another's story, ends up telling his own. Findley modeled Charlie's narration on Nick's in Fitzgerald's *The Great Gatsby*, where in recounting the story of Jay Gatsby's dream Nick reveals his own. The romanticized image of another person against whose idealization the narrator defines himself seems very much a creation of a preholocaust world. In his ongoing search for ways to survive the holocaust, Findley turns here to a world before it happened.

The novel opens with an isolated fragment in the first person set in the summer of 1910. This text is repeated near the end of the novel, when Charlie reveals that this is his mother's account of his own conception and her lament for what might have been with his father, indicated through the poignant and unfinished phrase, with its trailing ellipses: "If only . . ." (*Daughter*, 450). This phrase suggests that, like Fagan's fables as described in *Headhunter*, Findley's novel will record a fictional story that tells necessary truths about the world as he sees it. Findley's beginnings are usually shocking images of violent beauty, intensity, or black humor. This lyrical, gentle, and nostalgic image is equally memorable but surprising in its departure from Findley's usual mode. The "if only . . ." of Lily's lament is gently nostalgic for what might have been: a continuation of a perfect happiness. Later in the story, after Lily's collapse and incarceration, her mother Ede uses the same words, "if only," to mark her own "recrimination and guilt" (431). With this knowledge, this opening passage takes on a darker tinge, but the pantheistic idyll of Victorian romance remains the dominant tone.

Charlie begins his story proper in July 1939, the day after his mother Lily's death by fire in the Asylum for the Insane at Whitby, Ontario. Lily, who sees birth as a "flaming," describes her life and death in the same terms: "*I was struck like a match . . . I had no option but to burn*" (7). Charlie accepts her self-evaluation at face value. Like the fathers of Findley's mother and the fictional Cassandra Wakelin, Lily's stepfather, Frederick Wyatt, owns a piano factory, once "the largest piano manufacturing company in the British Empire" (8). The family fortunes are gone by 1939 but still provide a history and some money for their descendants. Whereas books and philosophy were as much the endangered species in *Headhunter*'s world as were dogs and birds, in *Daughter* the endangered species are pianos and the continuance in the Kilworth family line of what Lily calls "*the songs in the blood*" (9): the music of her inherited schizophrenia and pyromania.

Throughout the novel Charlie maintains that he will not risk passing on this defect; he will never allow a child of his to be conceived. But in the coda he reveals that a few years after he wrote this story, his wife gave birth to a daughter named Emma and he is glad. His acceptance of who his mother was and who his daughter might become is linked to a troubling price, however—his emasculation in the Second World War. After writing this story and going to war, Charlie is "altered—never to be the same" (459). His accident with the land mine mirrors his father's death in the First World War, and the story implies that somehow his disfigurement is connected to his fatherhood. He is no longer whole; he lives partly through his daughter now. With his injury, Charlie joins the ranks of Findley's other "broken dreamers." Like them, he knows that there is no safe place, but the final words of the novel affirm his faith in life itself and the bond life forges between human beings and the other species, a faith symbolized in the novel by Ede's field, where Charlie sets this affirmative conclusion to his story.

Like her grandmother before her, Charlie's daughter reaches out to the ants, and seeing the ant in her hands Charlie concludes, "We were not—and we will never be—alone" (461). These words circle around to the novel's epigraph from Oliver Sacks: "*It is their fate to be isolated and thus original.*" The novel affirms the validity of both statements. The mad, like Lily and her ancestor John Fagan, to whom the affliction or gift may first be traced, require recognition and accommodation of their difference, but they equally require acceptance of their full humanity in fellowship with the rest of the world. Humanity is judged by how it treats such special people. As a seven-year-old, Charlie disowned his mother in fear of her fits and what others might think of him because of them. To compensate for the betrayal of that day, he claims her in writing his book and sees the writing as a way of giving "her back her life" (12).

Cassandra's album of photographs is echoed in the album that Lily leaves as one of her "totems." These photographs challenge the passage of time, claiming "*This is me. This is us. This is now. Forever*" (15). They are the equivalent of the photograph of Robert Ross that concludes *The Wars* and of the words that Hugh Selwyn Mauberley has left on the walls, now remembered and preserved in the mind of Quinn in the novel *Famous Last Words*. But they are fragmented mementos of a broken past. The continuities have been severed. Through writing, both Charlie and Findley hope to reattach readers to the value of what has been lost. These actual photographs are accompanied by phantom photographs, as in *The Wars*, that record Charlie's mental memories as visual moments. He speaks of them as "a series of Lily-portraits that have no external counterpart" (235). They record Lily in her private moments with her box of matches and are her son's attempt to "conjure" understanding of his mother's complexity (236).

The pastoral scene of Charlie's conception outside Cambridge, with its "whispering chorus of insects," echoes Ede's field where Lily was both conceived and born. Ede's field is the symbol of that premodernist connection to the landscape and the natural world that the novel affirms as an ideal to which humanity must return if it is not to end in destruction.

The field sings Ede "[a] song about self. A song about place" (17). In the echo of Whitman, the language suggests the innocence of a new world where it is possible to begin again. The field shelters "all the mysteries of life" (18) and is opposed in Ede's mind to the Blakean *"dark, satanic mills"* of the city (120). When Lily meets Charlie's father, Karl Hess, the flautist and German soldier, she mistakes him for an incarnation of the field as "the great god Pan" of Elizabeth Barrett Browning's poem "A Musical Instrument" (451). The novel implies that writing is somewhat akin to music and madness: each endeavors to release trapped voices into song.

Music brings Ede together with Tom Wyatt, the piano man, who is later killed in an accident before he can learn of Lily's conception and marry Ede as he had planned. Charlie meets his wife, Alexandra, over the piano, when he is playing and she is singing in a band in 1936. He does not tell his mother about her nor her about his mother. As a result, Alexandra cannot understand his decision not to have children and their marriage breaks up for a time. His silence on these matters is never explained but suggests that his inability to become a husband and a father is linked to the intense attachment of love and shame that ties him to his mother.

Music also brought Lily together with Charlie's father, as Charlie reveals very late in his story through a confessional letter from one of his mother's best friends, who has also been the secret benefactor who sent Charlie to school. Coincidences such as this mark the novel's debt to Victorian generational sagas and Gothic romance. Charlie's citation of *David Copperfield* to mark both Lily's birth and his own alerts the reader to the shaping force of his imagination in the telling of the story and to the fact that, like Dickens's David, he is narrating his own life as much as his mother's. He shows Ede leaving the house to go to the field to give birth to Lily after closing *David Copperfield* at page 645 (20). Section five, which recounts Charlie's birth, is prefaced by another citation from Dickens's novel: *"I was a posthumous child"* (297). These citations, in drawing attention to Charlie's chosen models for framing his story, prepare the reader for the coincidences in the story he tells but they will not satisfy the reader unsympathetic to such devices. The form of the novel seems to be part of its nostalgic recycling of the past, but without the bitter edges of Findley's earlier works.

One of the most startling coincidences is Charlie's announcement that Lily's beloved friend Lizzie (Lisgard) Wyatt had died on the date of Charlie's birthday. Lizzie's unsuccessful brain surgery on a makeshift operating table in the kitchen is one of the great set scenes of the novel, praised by almost all the reviewers for its affecting melodrama. Charlie later confesses that he does not know when he was born (299). Lily chose to celebrate his birth in commemoration of Lizzie's death. In a further, extratextual coincidence, the date of Charlie's birth certificate, October 30, is Findley's birthday. This kind of play invites the reader to pay attention.

Lizzie, a lad full of love and life, is a young man so special he had been given a woman's name (257). Lily thinks of him as a "beautiful dreamer" (294). All that remains of him now is the photograph of Lizzie, Lily, and Lizzie's dog, Buster, "[t]ogether and alive" and smiling (296), a timeless image of vitality. This is close to being a parody of the photographic image that ends *The Wars*. Lizzie's death, with Tom's preceding it and Neddy's afterwards, mark the losses Lily seeks to fight with her fire. The music and beauty associated with these young men is wiped from the world as if their style of masculinity must yield to a grimmer model, that of the rigid brutality of Ede's husband, Frederick, patterned after Mr. Murdstone of *David Copperfield*. As Philip Marchand cynically comments: "In Findley's world, if you're a male, your chances of longevity are infinitely greater if you act like a repressed jerk."[3] These familiar Findley fates and mannerisms tread a fine line between sentimentality and genuine pathos. Marchand's suggestion that "Findley's own prose is sometimes infected by the over-blown histrionic quality of his characters" (Marchand, 416) ignores the fact that the novel is told in Charlie's voice, but the point remains valid in that Charlie's voice is the narrative. John Hulcoop, too, in another disappointed review, suggests that "[t]he piano tuner's voice needs retuning."[4] But is this perhaps the point? Charlie may have perfect pitch in identifying and replicating musical notes, but in human relations he has much to learn.

Charlie romanticizes his mother's life and her illness as Nick romanticizes Jay's dream in *The Great Gatsby*. This style of writing is currently out of fashion, at least with critics, although almost every review assumes that the masses will like it. Crossed with elements of the genealogical family saga in the style of Mazo de la Roche and the melodrama of high Victorian Gothic, Charlie's story, although entertaining, arouses misgivings in several reviewers. The timing of several of his key disclosures raises doubts about his reliability or even his competence as a narrator. Why does he delay announcing his reconciliation with his wife and the birth of his daughter until the coda? Why does he delay his account of his discovery of his father's identity until the end of his story when he returns to the details of his mother's death? These delays prolong suspense and ensure the telling of a good story, yet Findley's fiction usually offers more complex reasons for a narrator's decisions.

Charlie sees the larger horrors of the war framing his own family's tragedies even as he is aware that the magnitude of despair breaks fictional rules of balance. He writes: "Ten thousand men had died on the Somme in a single day. Multiply ten thousand men by ten thousand families and you can see how the tragedies mounted upwards" (*Daughter,* 417). He and Alexandra were married the day Guernica was bombed in 1937. He concludes, somewhat portentously, "The world—in every way—would never be the same" (238). This is all he says of his marriage day. Is he implying that even the happiest events are shadowed by the darkness of violence elsewhere, or is he implying some closer analogy between the two events? His grandmother's marriage was aborted by an accident and his mother's by the war. He has been voluble on the details of other consummations of which he has no firsthand knowledge, but he leaves his own wedding night a significant silence for readers to puzzle over.

He cross-frames his family saga, not just as Dickensian bildungsroman, gothic tale, and Fitzgeraldian elegiac romance, but also as a crosscast Shakespearean tragedy. It is a hybrid story that breaks every rule it invokes. After Ede has given birth, Charlie describes her as looking "like a female Lear returning from the heath" (61). Like Shakespeare's *King Lear,* this is a story of fathers and their children, but unlike *Lear*, the mothers are ultimately more important. As Charlie comments, "There are so many fathers in this story . . . they have only one thing in common: their habit of disappearing" (62). Like Lear, Ede gives up her kingdom (the field) and command of herself to go into the city and give herself in marriage to a tyrant, Frederick Wyatt, the brother of the piano man, Tom. She betrays her daughter, allowing her to be locked in the attic by her husband, but she does not disappear. She endures while Frederick eventually fades. Despite her complicities, she remains a locus of hope for the future in her commitment to life and her capacity for wonder.

Frederick is shamed by Lily's fits and her pyromania, and Ede, her spirit already broken by her marriage to a man brutal and rigid in his pursuit of propriety, does not protest. According to her grandson, she pays for mere survival with her integrity (177). Lily alone is blamed for her inherited condition. The dark secret within the family of an imperfect child marks its fundamental instability as a unit capable of offering children the safety they need to grow up into the world with confidence.

The hypocrisy of lying about the reality of who constitutes the family inducts children into lying when they should be raised to cherish the truth. In these ways, the lies and cruelties within the family mirror the larger society these families combine to create. In *The Wars,* Robert senses that there is a connection between his rape and Rowena's portrait in that they both attest to the lies of an authority that betrays the trust it is sworn to protect. Charlie identifies the same darkness at the heart of his own family's history, and sees it reflected in the world wars that define the twentieth century. The darkness is not the madness itself, which is seen as both a blessing and a curse, but the silencing and repression of that truth.

Ede's mother, Eliza, who has not told the story of their ancestor mad John Fagan, even to her husband, eventually tells Ede when Lily's condition can no longer be denied. John Fagan too was locked in the attic by parents who were ashamed of his special gifts. He created the equivalent of Ede's field on the walls of the attic, painting and writing God's message on the walls *"like an illuminated manuscript. All the capital letters were decorated with leaves and bees and singing birds"* (115). One whole wall depicts flames. The equivalent of Mauberley's testament on the walls of *Famous Last Words,* John Fagan's creation reminds readers of the fine line tread between madness and creativity. Like Lilah and her mentor, John's descendant Nicholas Fagan, John too treads this line. One day the Dublin house burnt to the ground with Uncle John and most of his family in it. History repeats itself, but in a pattern of sameness and difference. This is Lily's heritage, and Charlie's, and, by implication, the world's: joy and grief, creativity and destruction, inextricably intertwined. Far from being marginal or extraneous to humanity, this creative violence is the essence of being human, a doubled sign of mortality and infinity.

At her most intense, Lily evokes this signature Findley vision at its most compelling, but at other times she seems simply the madcap, spoiled schoolgirl of silly infatuations who lives only for the fleeting satisfactions of a life of aimless pleasure: her son's memories of her at her happiest are of singing, dancing, and movie-going, with the occasional offer of her body to unhappy strangers. In her pleasures she embodies the dissipations of the "Lost Generation" of the 1920s just as in her terrors she represents the violence of the two world wars between which the twenties are too brief an interlude.

By fixing his account of his mother on paper, Charlie ensures she will never take him by surprise again. He has reversed the power dynamic of their relationship. Where she once led and he followed, he has now assumed the writer's power to control what gets recorded and how it is remembered. Charlie seems ready at last to be a proper husband to his wife and father to his daughter, except for that troubling, Hemingwayesque war wound that suggests his long-suffering wife will continue to be shortchanged, as she is in this narrative of his life. Her compelling desire to have a child is Alexandra's only reason for existence in this story. Every other dimension of her being is absent. Charlie's obsession with his origins and with a lost past of genteel Edwardian pastoral suggests a man old before his time and ill-adapted to the postwar world awaiting him. He has lived vicariously through his mother, and now seems prepared to live the rest of his life through his daughter. As a narrator, he manipulates the power of narrative to create suspense and control the unfolding of time, but as a person he seems both literally and metaphorically impotent: a living testimony to the damage children suffer when neglected by their parents.

I see Charlie's story as part of a collection of narratives centered on the notion of impotence that also includes *The Last of the Crazy People, You Went Away, The Stillborn Lover,* and the Bragg and Minna stories. With *The Butterfly Plague,* Findley initiated a lengthy examination of power that reached its culmination in *Headhunter.* With *The Piano Man's Daughter* he returns to his earliest theme—impotence—with a matured understanding of its complexity.

The Impotence of Childhood

Charlie's impotence in the face of his mother's madness is mirrored in *You Went Away* by Matthew's inability to influence the course of his parents' disintegrating marriage. *You Went Away* is preceded by a short prologue that begins with the discovery of an unlabeled box of photographs at the flea market. One photograph in particular invites speculation: a man and a woman walking away from the camera in the rain. There are so many possible stories embedded here but *"there is nothing here of certainty."*[5] As the nameless narrator shuffles through the box, the voice seeks to make connections among these fragments, which seem *"a patchwork of unstitched lives"* (*Away,* 4). Here is the narrative situation initiated in *The Wars* and echoed in *Daughter.* In this text it introduces the story of nine-year-old Matthew Forbes, whose father, Graeme, leaves his wife, Michael, and his children to enlist in the air force, hoping to fight in the Second World War.

The story, told by a puzzled narrator groping through the fragments of the box, reconstructs with growing confidence a focus on Matthew's perspective, beginning in September 1939 at his grandmother's house as the family sits in front of her mantelpiece, a photographic shrine to the family dead from the First World War: her husband and older son. Graeme, her youngest son and Matthew's father, survived the war, being just 15. Graeme's mother, Ellen, does not "seem to approve of his survival. His picture was not on the mantel with the heroes" (8). Deprived of his own father by one war, Graeme's need to be a hero and his failure to fulfill that role lead him to abandon his own son to a similar dispossession.

Like Robert's mother in *The Wars,* the grandmother Ellen vents her impotent rage at the powers that have deprived her family of men through war: "If there is a God—He's mad. I renounce Him" (9). Graeme, in contrast, is jubilant at the chance to enter what he thinks of as an athletic contest, a chance to shine, and happily leaves his family behind without a thought for them. The rest of the story explores the gap in responses to the war between husband and wife, father and son. The triangle of desire linking mother, father, and son is eventually broken by Graeme's increasing callousness, to be replaced by a new triangle of mother, lover, and son. But the lover, also the product of a broken home, is in his own way as self-destructive as Graeme. At the end of the book the only bond left is the unspoken sympathy of shared and thwarted desire linking mother and son.

Where the father sees in war an opportunity to shed the responsibilities of family and embrace his freedom as an individual, seeking to recapture his youthful promise as a potential hero, his wife and children experience the emotional and financial pain of his absence. On Matthew's birthday, instead of the bike his father had promised him, Graeme gives him the news of his imminent departure, expecting his son to be as pleased as he is. This is only the first of a series of disappointments Matthew must endure from his irresponsible father. When his mother is forced to sell their belongings, Matthew hides one figure marked "NOT FOR SALE" in a vain attempt to keep at least some things the same (29).

But he discovers that time cannot be frozen. Nothing is said, but Matthew learns through overhearing conversations and snooping in drawers that his father has been demoted because of his drinking problem and womanizing, and later that he will not be sent to the front as he had wished but has been assigned a desk job. He can never be a hero. Matthew's younger sister, Bonnie, is killed in a freak accident while her parents are preoccupied with the disintegration of their own relationship. Her death loses meaning in the context of the war, "where men and women were just statistics" (47). This incredibly bleak portrait of empty lives and the misery of abandonment deals Michael and Matthew blow after blow. He is banished to the misery of boarding school and his mother to her mother-in-law's house. The family has no home.

The disintegration of the family is paralleled by the progress of the war, but the analogies drawn between Graeme's impotence in bed with Michael and the fall of Singapore (87), and between France's fall and Michael's impulse to surrender in the war to hang on to Graeme (88), seem inappropriate except as indicators of how claustrophobic this couple's lives have become as Graeme's self-destructive fall pulls down the whole family with him. The family's dependence on this undependable man highlights the vulnerability of women in this world, as Michael's friend Eloise points out, and especially of children (91). The cruelty of Matthew's father is breathtaking. Family life is portrayed as a series of acts of petty meanness and betrayal.

The only happy people who offer Matthew and Michael the gifts of wonder and kindness are single: the eccentric Miss Nella Mott, who reminds Matthew of his best friend, Rupert, from school, and Ivan Henderson, who had fled an alcoholic, abusive father to join the air force, and who, after trying to help Graeme and befriending his family, begins an affair with Michael. The truly intense relationship, however, is Matthew's transference of desire from his father to Ivan. Nella and Ivan have retained their capacity for wonder. But like all of Findley's beautiful young men in love with distance, Ivan is doomed. His plane falls from the sky like Icarus, but to Matthew and the narrator he is still Pegasus, the potent flying horse of Greek mythology (202, 218).

The night before Ivan's death Matthew experiences an erotic dream in which he flies naked through the sky with Ivan on his motorcycle, which he associates with the flying horse, Pegasus. It is a wet dream that ends with the fall of the motorcycle, as if such love can only be consummated in death. The next day, Ivan insists on going up in his plane alone with the intention of breaking "every rule in the book" (205). He thinks of it as "dancing with danger" (205) because he too wants to leave Michael and Matthew behind to be sent overseas into the arena of war. In such transgression he finds an exhilarating freedom. The sky for him is a "playing field" (205). But the wings of the plane fall off, as Icarus's wings failed him in the Greek legend. Ivan is not the Pegasus of heroes but the mortal punished for hubris.

With Ivan's death, the story of Matthew's growing up seems ended. Ivan is the hero in Matthew's mind that Graeme failed to become, but in Findley's fictional world such heroes and such objects of desire cannot live. In the terms of Findley's earlier play, Ivan is another "stillborn lover." The accusatory lament of the title, "you went away," which at first seems addressed to the absent father, is now transferred to the ideal lover. It is the cry of the abandoned would-be lover, a cry of impotence and loss.

Stillborn Desires

As Harry Lane explains in a superb analysis of *The Stillborn Lover,* "The play's overt action is an interrogation regarding possible betrayal of country, but it also conducts a counter-interrogation focusing on betrayal of truth, and of self."[6] In balancing the two, as so often in Findley's work, the emotional weight of the play falls on personal identity and betrayals, giving insufficient attention, in my view, to familial, professional, and social responsibilities.

Ambassador Harry Raymond has been recalled from the Soviet Union for interrogation regarding the murder of a young Russian boy. There are compromising photographs of his encounters with Mischa that have been supplied to the Canadian government by the KGB. The RCMP need to determine if Raymond has been blackmailed by the Russians into acting as a secret agent and if he is the murderer of Mischa. The situation is further complicated by the political ambitions of Raymond's friend Michael Riordan, the man who appointed him to the position and who is now preparing to run for election as prime minister of Canada. Riordan cannot afford to publicly back his friend but searches for a compromise that might save public embarrassment for everyone.

Raymond, thinking only of himself, feels betrayed because Riordan is not willing to jeopardize his career to support him. But Riordan now realizes that Raymond is a man he never really knew because he was not allowed access to Raymond's secret self. The friendship has been revealed as hollow, not just because of Riordan's ambitions, which have always been public, but also because of Raymond's secretiveness about what he considers his private life. In asking whether a public figure can have a private life, the play seems to endorse, through Raymond's special pleading, a view of life in which public and private should be completely severed. Yet the accompanying images and memories of the Raymonds' time in Japan at the end of the Second World War work against such a view, leaving the reader or audience in a position of stalemate. Raymond's generation is responsible for the holocausts of the bombs dropped on Japan, yet, despite their class privilege and access to power, they feel impotent to influence the course of history.

These semipublic revelations in the safe house question sessions with the RCMP of what he has hidden all his life prompt Raymond to "come out" with defiant pride to his friend and his daughter. He now seems to regret his much earlier decision never to act on his desires, a decision made when he first fell in love with a young man at Cambridge, Francis Oliver, who shortly afterward was killed in the Spanish Civil War and lost to him forever. Raymond reveals that it was his relationship with the beautiful poet Oliver that prompted his decision "[t]o live incognito." Oliver once said to him, " 'You are my stillborn lover' "[7] Although he married his wife Marian with the resolve that his homosexual desire would be forever stillborn, she has seen his need and encouraged him to indulge it, even to the extent of procuring him young men, including Mischa. Her well-intentioned act has now brought on disaster.

The play raises serious moral and political issues involving the behavior of the Canadian government and security forces during the Cold War period when witch-hunts against suspected communists and homosexuals ruined many innocent lives. Lane explains that Findley modeled Raymond's story on the details of the harassment of two Canadian diplomats, John Watkins and Herbert Norman, both of who were cleared of the charges against them but died as a result of the harassment. Unfortunately, the portrayal of Raymond distracts attention from these questions of public accountability to focus instead on the internal contradictions of a deeply troubled man.

Raymond is another of Findley's orphans, whose parents died when he was six. The play endorses his self-presentation as a kind of tragically compromised hero, someone who has never been able to be himself. His problem is not his sexual orientation but his own secrecies and compromises around it, as manifested in the ill-advised decision to have sex with a prostitute of foreign nationality whose identity he does not know. Even worse, perhaps, is his subsequent refusal to take responsibility for these actions. It is hypocritical of him at this stage in his life to accuse his daughter of not knowing him because she does not want to know who he is as a homosexual. On the page, it is possible to read these lines sympathetically but hearing and seeing them on stage they ring false. Raymond is a desperate man trying to blame others for his own inadequacies. Not only is he incapable of understanding or caring about the repercussions of his actions for his country's welfare and international diplomacy, but he cannot even see that a father's lying to his daughter may well have an effect on her. He tells her, "This is not something that happened to you, Diana. It happened to me. And to your mother" (*Lover,* 55). At some level, the play implies that such blindness marks the failure of a generation of parents, but that implication works against the sympathy it struggles to create for Harry as a newly self-declared homosexual.

An encounter with his friend Riordan enacts a similar attempt for Raymond to evade his own responsibility in the disaster now enveloping him. Raymond accuses Riordan of cutting him loose because he cannot afford to know him: to know him, it is implied, as a homosexual, not as a loose cannon. He says, "It doesn't matter—does it—that I did not betray your trust. That I was loyal to my posting and to my country" (86). In fact, however, he did betray his friend's trust, by not informing him of his sexual orientation, which in that context at that time did constitute a liability. He further betrayed his posting by engaging in sex with Mischa, knowing such activity laid him open to blackmail. He was in a position of national trust and betrayed that trust. I see the problem less as one of sexual orientation than one of judgment. However one looks at it, the affair with Mischa was an act of bad judgment, not because it was homosexual but because it rendered Raymond potentially ineffectual as a diplomat in a situation requiring tact and discretion.

By showing Raymond and Riordan privileging the personal above their public responsibilities, and by having only the unsympathetic RCMP officer speak of the public interest, Findley loads the dice in favor of the personal, which is already the preferred mode of understanding in North American culture today. On the other hand, the wealth and privilege of the setting, and the assumption of social entitlement that leads the Raymonds to expect special treatment and to despise the officers running the interrogation, works against creating sympathy for their self-created dilemma on the stage. By making Raymond a self-indulgent old man who has betrayed his friend's trust, his wife and daughter's love, and his own self-image of who he tried to be, Findley creates another problematically complicit figure for understanding.

Lane's analysis insightfully identifies the ways in which, "[b]eneath the witty, self-protective dialogue exist various kinds of panic" (Lane, 445). Ostensibly a play attacking the homosexual panic of the authorities, the drama puts its emotional energies into the frustrated triangulated desires of Harry, Marian, Diana, and an ideal "stillborn lover" of their imaginations. Harry and Marian have lived their lives with the idealized "stillborn lover" a gap and a link between them. Diana is unable to form a lasting relationship with a man because her idealized image of her father (based on the lie of who he is) interferes as a "stillborn lover" preventing the formation of an actual attachment to a real man.

Their impotence is framed by the Japanese Game of Go, whose rules are described in the prelude and coda of the play. The ritual moves of the game ensure that "[o]nce the stones have been set in place, they cannot be withdrawn. Their positions are locked, irrevocable. Like the moves and gestures we make with our lives" (prelude). The coda reports that when the game is over the loser approaches the Master, asking "Where did I go wrong?" The Master always replies: "Everywhere" (coda). This may be read as another variation on Findley's recurrent admonition to "pay attention." The reminder that the repercussions of some decisions must be lived with forever can encourage a greater cherishing of the agency people do have or a refusal to act at all for fear of making the wrong decision. But then not acting is also an act with a cost, as Harry Raymond learns. His first fatal move was to cast himself as a "stillborn lover." In contrast, his wife Marian swings out over the ravine in a manner reminiscent of Ivan's dangerous flying in *You Went Away.* Her flirting with danger and his fear of attachment have proved a deadly combination, but despite their failures, they have maintained a connection that lasts to the end. There is affirmation in their acceptance of each other in their strengths and their weaknesses. In their final moments, the play identifies a source of strength in their unconventional marriage that is also a recurring theme in the Bragg and Minna stories. For Raymond and Marian, however, the only way left them to assert who they are lies in choosing death.

Immortal Mortality

Findley has published three books of short stories, each collection loosely connected through its title but all producing variations of the invocation and survival of images of holocaust. *Dinner along the Amazon,* like *Headhunter,* examines the darkness behind civilizational veneers of politeness and convention. It turns the anthropological gaze, once reserved for others, back onto the Western civilization that invented it. Many of the stories are told in the first person, creating a variety of voices from the inside, yet all the narrators, male and female, share the puzzled distress of people who feel themselves somehow outsiders trying to makes sense of impulses in themselves and others that can hardly be articulated because the language to describe them is still being invented.

Although each story stands on its own, several reveal the seeds of later, more extended works. "Lemonade," in its lengthy evocation of nine-year-old Harper Dewey's half-comprehending anguish over his mother's retreat into alcoholism and in the crazy logic of his response seems an early study for Hooker Winslow. "The People on the Shore," told by a character named "Tiff" (Findley's nickname), recounts a death on the beach of a hotel in Maine that provides a variation on the themes elaborated in *The Telling of Lies*. "Dinner along the Amazon" introduces some of the themes and names that recur differently distributed in *Headhunter*. What Olivia thinks of as "the tidy horror of what was really going to happen" (*Dinner,* 234) in the story becomes in the novel a flooding tide of horror gone completely beyond control. A character named Conrad arranges the odd gathering for the revelatory dinner party in "Dinner" just as the author Conrad provides the scenario for *Headhunter*. In "Hello Cheeverland, Goodbye," the filtering consciousness of a young man readers are told to call "Ishmael" implicitly contrasts the epic passions of *Moby Dick* with the messy but banal horrors of wealthy American suburbia as detailed by Cheever.

"Daybreak at Pisa" is a scene between Ezra and Dorothy Pound that was eventually omitted from the final version of *The Trials of Ezra Pound*. "Out of the Silence," a play in progress, depicts T. S. Eliot (here called Tom) raiding his wife Vivien's dreams, stealing her voice, having her committed, and finally appropriating her death for his poetry. These sketches stage Findley's interrogation of the ethics and gender politics of modernism's privileging of the controlling artist through the unhappy marriages of these famous men. The sexual triangles of desire depicted in "Sometime—Later—Not Now" and "Losers, Finders, Strangers at the Door" also consider the complex interdependencies of personal relationships within the contexts of sixties bohemianism and outwardly respectable suburban solitude, respectively. Many of these characters court danger and are sometimes broken as a result.

In style, the futuristic horror of "What Mrs. Felton Knew" seems to stand apart from the other stories in *Dinner* in its horrific account of holocaust visited upon the contented farms of America, but thematically it makes articulate the lives of quiet dread, suppressed panic, and desolated loneliness depicted in the rest of the collection. Each of these stories shares an obsession with surviving the holocaust, which is sometimes an external and sometimes an internal devastation of dreams. Some characters actively flee it whereas others welcome it into themselves. "Hello Cheeverland, Goodbye" shows people vainly seeking protection in money when the fires that are consuming the poorer districts have already symbolically reached them. "About Effie" shows Effie innocently anticipating apocalypse as an ultimate spiritual and sexual fulfillment, and "Losers, Finders, Strangers at the Door" speaks the anguish of a woman inviting a messenger of apocalypse (as sadomasochistic triangulated desire) into her home rather than having it ambush her marriage elsewhere. "Out of the Silence" shows the creative artist milking his wife's personal immolation in the fires of an internally experienced holocaust for creative inspiration and his own public acclaim.

The Bud and Neil Cable stories, begun here, continue in the collection *Stones* as the narrator, Neil, explores his relationships with his brother, Bud, and his father through a series of traumatic moments. "War" explains a family photo taken just before his father went into the army when Neil was 10. Neil learns from his brother that his father has joined the army without telling him. Feeling betrayed, angry, and hurt, he throws stones at his father when he arrives to say good-bye but cannot explain his mixed emotions or his actions. The photograph records the family posing as if united for the father to carry away an image that fails to capture the complexity of that day. Neil can see where the stones he threw have marked his father's face, but his own wounds are not visible. The stones of this story, collected as gifts, are turned to weapons with which Neil tries to speak the anguish he cannot articulate. The gap he cannot close with words is closed with violence.

The Neil and Bud stories in *Stones* adopt the form of elegiac romance as Neil tells his own story of guilt, betrayal, and personal inadequacies, ostensibly through telling Bud's. Alcoholism is the holocaust that visits Bud in "The Name's the Same," but it is the symptom rather than the cause of his troubles. "Real Life Writes Real Bad" reveals Bud as another broken dreamer, consumed by dreams he cannot fulfill. Like so many of Findley's characters, "Bud wanted out of being who he was" (*Stones,* 155). He cannot meet his own dreams of glory, symbolized by his cherishing of *The Great Gatsby.* Like a true colonial, he moves from Toronto to London, England, seeking instant glory, but he must return to Canada, defeated and still looking for the impossible. Neil calls him a "desperado" (154), romanticizing his "psychic withdrawal" (158) as a form of specialness that Neil has been unable to support. Comparing the sordid banality of "Bud and Katie's tragedy" to the "mad and alcoholic heroes" of the great modernist tradition, Neil concludes: *"real life writes real bad. It should take lessons from the masters"* (170). Through Neil's irony, Findley both notes his debts to these precursors and marks his difference. Their visions don't fulfill his perception of the contradictions of reality, the inadequacies of such images of manhood and heroism, and the dangers in glorifying self-destruction.

Each story in *Stones* examines the fate individuals are dealt, its weight, its hardness, its solidity, as if it were made of the stones in the Game of Go. If mortality is a stone in the stories of *Stones,* the stories of *Dust to Dust* promise that even stones disintegrate eventually. These two collections are preoccupied with mortality. Mortality, they demonstrate, is at once a source of vulnerability, glory, and despair. These stories are littered with the bodies of broken dreamers and the sorrowing of those who loved them, but in the telling of their stories there is remembrance and reconciliation.

Stones opens and closes with the scattering of ashes at significant places where public and private memories converge. Each ending opens up another beginning. In "Bragg and Minna," Minna's ashes are scattered by her husband and lovers at a petroglyph created by aborigines in Australia depicting a celebration of every form of life. Bragg and Minna had parted over the birth of their child, Stella. Bragg had never wanted a child, fearing they might create a monster, but Minna, who does not share his fear of monstrosity, insists. Stella is born with deformities, as if to give embodiment to Bragg's deepest fears.

In learning to accept Stella's "monstrosity," Bragg finds himself reconciled to his own. The death ritual converts Bragg to Minna's views, and their long battles, depicted through a series of stories, end with a reconciliation that extends from Bragg's love for Minna to his acceptance of the child and of himself.

The collection ends with "Stones," the story of a son, Ben Max, scattering the ashes of his father, David, at the scene of the battle of Dieppe. David, never able to forgive himself for his failure of nerve at Dieppe, returned to his family a broken and violent man, incapable of giving or receiving love. The family lived a nightmare as a result, yet the story records a son's love and forgiveness for a life gone terribly wrong. At Dieppe Ben is able to close the circle, marking a conclusion to his father's agony at the place where it began. He ends his story back in Toronto, however, insisting that the authorities, in the person of Colonel Matheson, cannot ignore the existence of his family. The Maxes are the shopkeepers who serve the privileged and who bear the brunt of the tragedies of war. Ben's version of Dieppe and its aftermath challenges the official story and will not be silenced.

The second story in the collection, "A Gift of Mercy," documents the meeting and marriage of Bragg and Minna, in which Minna gives herself as a gift of mercy to Bragg, thinking, "[W]hy were the lost so beautiful?" (32). Bragg thinks that she is mad, and also beautiful. For a time they live and write their books together, balancing her fascination with the homeless and the mad against his with beautiful young men. When Minna invites a homeless woman into her bed and forces her way into Bragg's bed (using the excuse that her own bed is occupied), Bragg responds by bringing a young man home to his bed. Minna thinks: *"We've come full circle from the day we met and now our lives will never be the same"* (57). By placing this chronologically earlier story second in the collection, Findley reinforces his belief that every end may also be a beginning.

The heart of the book is devoted to a series of chronicles of highly individuated and harrowing nervous breakdowns experienced primarily from the inside: "Foxes," "The Sky," and "Dreams." These are stories of metamorphoses: a fox takes over the body of a man in a chillingly enigmatic story, one of Findley's best; paranoia consumes a businessman in a black comedy of social satire; a violent schizophrenic stores the bloodied bodies he has murdered and mutilated in the dreams of his psychiatrist, whose wife, also a psychiatrist, shares the horror in an effort to carry him through it. As professional watchers, they have been invaded by what they have watched. She has lost an autistic child, who has chosen to die rather than respond to the surveillance and care of his keepers. Now her husband's patient is taking revenge of a different kind. Boundaries between self and other are broken down in terrifying ways that force the reader to reconceptualize reality. This story recalls Michel Foucault's analysis of the dynamics of the psychiatric investigation, which functions as a mechanism "with a double impetus: pleasure and power. The pleasure that comes of exercising a power that questions, monitors . . . and on the other hand, the pleasure that kindles at having to evade this power . . . The power that lets itself be invaded by the pleasure it is pursuing; and opposite it, power asserting itself in the pleasure of showing off, scandalising, or resisting." For Foucault, such interactions are "not boundaries not to be crossed, but perpetual spirals of power and pleasure."[8] This strikes me as an excellent description of how Findley's investigations of violence, thwarted desires, and various forms of madness operate. The reader is cast in the position of the investigating psychiatrist probing these conditions, and, like Dr. Menilow of "Dreams," seduced into a participation that provides experiences of power and pleasure.

The pleasures of horror, revulsion, and self-recognition may be cathartic or troubling. Harrowing as the experience is, Findley suggests that these personal holocausts may show the way to preventing public holocausts of the future. Through reading, readers may break down those boundaries between the known and the unknown, self and other, in potentially liberating ways even as, in Foucault's terms, they participate in the unfolding spirals of pleasure and power. By inviting the strangers of these texts into their imaginations, as Minna invites street people into her home and her fictions, readers may learn to conquer their fears of difference in the world they inhabit outside the text and to come to terms with their own internal ambivalences.

Dust to Dust recapitulates the themes and style that defines the Findley fictional world. Two more Bragg and Minna stories work through the themes encapsulated in their unconventional marriage. "A Bag of Bones" explores more deeply Bragg's fear of children and Minna's desire for them. "Come as You Are" addresses the need for self-acceptance and the tyranny of narrowly prescribed definitions of masculine identity. They appear at the heart of the collection, preceded by three stories of untimely death, three suicides and a murder, and followed by four stories that more specifically address the theme of holocausts, both past and future.

The opening and closing stories are among Findley's most haunting. Each implies that we are all responsible for the deaths that occur among us. Inattention and ignorance are no excuse. "Dust" opens with a demonic child killing a cat. By the time the story ends with the boy's death by drowning, an apparent suicide as plea for attention, the reader has come to understand that the child's monstrosity was a desperate call for help as his parents' marriage fell apart and neither had time to attend to him. As a retelling of Aesop's fable "The Boy Who Cried Wolf," the story problematizes certainty about the moral of this illustrative story, implying that judgment of the boy may have come too quickly. The citizens who ignored his cries, assuming they meant nothing, were not only wrong, they were derelict in their duty in attending to their fellow citizen. "The Madonna of the Cherry Trees," the volume's final story, makes this latter point explicit through its open critique of the communal silences that enabled concentration camps to exist in peaceful French villages during the war while the citizens consoled themselves that "[i]t was not us" (*Dust,* 223). This story returns to the question of justifications for murder first raised in *The Last of the Crazy People* and continued in *The Telling of Lies*. Indeed, Vanessa Van Horne returns in a stylish detective story, "Abracadaver," in which the motive for murder is also connected to collaboration with the enemy during the war.

"Hilton Agonistes" is a disturbing satire that situates the holocaust in a revolution against neocolonial rule on a Caribbean island. The story focuses on the plight of an ordinary middle-aged Canadian couple, Nicholas and Nicole Halifax, who narrowly miss being massacred while staying at the Hilton. The story ends as they try to wait out the revolution in deck chairs on the beach as murder and mayhem continue back at the hotel they have fled. As an allegory for how Canadians as a nationality appear to think that they can ignore the foundations of their privilege on repressions elsewhere, the story is devastating. As so often in Findley, the hotel symbolizes a garrisoned form of life of sheltered luxury that promises asylum but proves not to be immune to the history of the world that breaks down its doors. This couple's smug assurance that Canada is the best of all possible worlds and that they themselves are not racist is undercut by their own dialogue and behavior. The story comes to no conclusion, as if to suggest that the verdict is still out: Canadians have time to examine themselves and their society more closely and to recognize that their involvement in the world outside Canada's borders must embrace a stronger commitment to social justice than can be expressed by a two-week holiday in the sun. In the context of other stories more explicitly addressing the moral deficiencies of collaboration and complicity in oppression through silence or inaction, this story suggests that the privileged ignorance of this Canadian couple is as dangerous as the active evil of the vicious women who are murdered by their victim's friend in "The Madonna of the Cherry Trees." The faith of Nicholas and Nicole that their definition of normality will prevail is the last pathetic gasp of the idea of Empire, and all too terribly human. As symbols, they represent a type of moral bankruptcy, but as individuated human beings they deserve attention and a certain respect. They exist multidimensionally, as people and as symbols.

Taken as a whole, these stories continue in their own ways to cry Wolf, harassing an audience inured to prophecies of doom to continue to pay attention to the holocausts in our history and the potential holocausts to come. Many of these stories brilliantly position readers to identify against their conditioned impulses as a way of destabilizing certainties about what everyone knows. Findley's work can be predictable in the dilemmas it presents and the imagery through which it develops them, but it continues to surprise in the variety and eloquence through which it celebrates and marvels at the contradictions of life.

Many critics see their job as trying to categorize Findley's work. He sees his job as evading categorization. Although his narrators often try to make sense of the broken pieces of history and his characters often hold up talismans or totems of such fragments as sources of meaning in a universe characterized only by meaninglessness, Findley's fiction itself does not create the order one would expect from a modernist text. Neither does he celebrate a total relativity of values as a postmodernist might. I have suggested that Findley's approach to understanding reality derives from an angle of vision suspicious of centralizing systems, which may owe something to his experience as a Canadian and a homosexual of a certain generation but which he has crafted into a distinctively evocative style of his own. Findley breaks most of the rules dictated to creative writing students as a formula for success. His novels overflow with characters; his narrative forms are hybrid; he tells and shows and tells again; his prose is peppered with italics, ellipses, and short sentence fragments. And it all works beautifully. Findley's fictions insist that emotion matters, that emotional excess can be a virtue and not a sin in men and in women, and that the world depends on readers' abilities to immerse themselves in strange new worlds and come away transformed.

One scene from *Inside Memory* has always haunted me. Findley spends the night in the pen with his dogs in an effort to understand their private lives from their own perspectives. In the morning, he is astonished to discover that they rise to bow to the sun at the "exact moment" of its emergence over the horizon (*Memory*, 102). In their honoring of the sun, they teach him an attitude to life that is lost to modernism and postmodernism alike. It is closer to the teachings of the earth celebrated by native writers. Indeed, Ojibway writer Ruby Slipperjack has published a novel called *Honour the Sun*. Findley's intuitive attentiveness to the lessons of where he lives and the companions with whom he lives translates into fiction that seeks a form of nonrepressive "reconciliation" that can best be achieved through the creative collaborations inaugurated by the reading and writing of books (*Memory*, 305).

Notes and References

Preface

    1. Timothy Findley, "Stones," in *Stones* (New York: Viking, 1988), 198; this and other stories from this collection are hereafter cited in text as *Stones*.

    2. Paul de Man, *Blindness and Insight: Essays in the Rhetoric of Contemporary Criticism* (Minneapolis: University of Minnesota Press, 1983), 148.

    3. Timothy Findley, *Headhunter* (Toronto: HarperCollins, 1993), 386; hereafter cited in text as *Headhunter.*

Chapter One

    1. Laurie Kruk, "I Want Edge: An Interview with Timothy Findley," *Canadian Literature* 148 (Spring 1996): 126; hereafter cited in text.

    2. Timothy Findley, introduction to *Dinner along the Amazon* (New York: Penguin, 1984), x; this collection hereafter cited in text as *Dinner.*

    3. Simon During, *Patrick White* (Melbourne: Oxford University Press, 1996), 26.

    4. Lorraine York, *Front Lines: The Fiction of Timothy Findley* (Toronto: ECW, 1991), xii; hereafter cited in text.

    5. Donna Palmateer Pennee, *Moral Metafiction: Counter-discourse in the Novels of Timothy Findley* (Toronto: ECW, 1991), 11; hereafter cited in text.

    6. Anne Geddes Bailey, *Dangerous Acts: Intertextual Ambivalence in the Novels of Timothy Findley* (Vancouver: Talonbooks, in press).

    7. Tom Hastings, "Into the Fire: Masculinities and Militarism in Timothy Findley's *The Wars*" (Ph.D. diss., York University, 1997), 59.

    8. Barbara Gabriel, "Staging Monstrosity: Genre, Life-Writing, and Timothy Findley's *The Last of the Crazy People*," *Essays on Canadian Writing* 54 (Winter 1994):170; hereafter cited in text.

    9. Carol Roberts, *Timothy Findley: Stories from a Life* (Toronto: ECW, 1994), 11; hereafter cited in text.

    10. Timothy Findley, "Dust," *Dust to Dust: Stories* (Toronto: HarperCollins, 1997), 28; this and other stories from this collection hereafter cited as *Dust.*

    11. Johan Aitken, " 'Long Live the Dead': An Interview with Timothy Findley," *Journal of Canadian Fiction* 33 (1981–1982): 88.

    12. Timothy Findley, *Inside Memory: Pages from a Writer's Workbook* (Toronto: HarperCollins, 1990), 19; hereafter cited as *Memory.*

    13. Mary Jane Miller, "An Analysis of *The Paper People*," *Canadian Drama* 9, no. 1 (1983): 56.

14. Timothy Findley, "Alice Drops Her Cigarette on the Floor . . . (William Whitehead looking over Timothy Findley's Shoulder)," *Canadian Literature* 91 (Winter 1981): 11–12; hereafter cited in text as "Alice."

15. Timothy Findley, introduction to *The Butterfly Plague*, rev. ed. (Markham, Ontario: Penguin, 1986), iv; hereafter cited in text as *Plague*. All subsequent quotations are from this edition of the text unless otherwise stated.

16. Donald Cameron, "Timothy Findley: Make Peace with Nature, Now," *Conversations with Canadian Novelists*, volume 1 (Toronto: Macmillan, 1973), 52; hereafter cited in text.

Chapter Two

1. Timothy Findley, *The Last of the Crazy People* (Toronto: Macmillan Laurentian Library, 1977), 99; hereafter cited in text as *Crazy*.

2. Simon Gikandi, *Maps of Englishness: Writing Identity in the Culture of Colonialism* (New York: Columbia University Press, 1996), 3.

3. Graeme Gibson, "Timothy Findley," in *Eleven Canadian Novelists* (Toronto: Anansi, 1973), 145; hereafter cited in text.

4. Nancy Huston, "Novels and Navels," *Critical Inquiry* 21 (Summer 1995): 713.

5. Northop Frye, *The Bush Garden: Essays on the Canadian Imagination* (Toronto: Anansi, 1971), 220.

6. Toni Morrison, *Playing in the Dark: Whiteness and the Literary Imagination* (Cambridge, Mass. and London: Harvard University Press, 1992), 57.

7. Homi Bhabha, "Sly Civility," in *The Location of Culture* (New York and London: Routledge, 1994), 93–101.

8. Norah Storey, "Family Compact," in *The Oxford Companion to Canadian History and Literature* (Toronto: Oxford University Press, 1967), 248.

9. Jonathan Dollimore, *Sexual Dissidence: Augustine to Wilde, Freud to Foucault* (Oxford: Clarendon, 1991), 11, 17; hereafter cited in text.

10. *Globe and Mail* (Toronto), 25 Nov 1993, D9.

11. Moe Meyer, "Introduction: Reclaiming the Discourse of Camp," in *The Politics and Poetics of Camp*, ed. Moe Meyer (New York: Routledge, 1994), 1.

12. Timothy Findley, *The Butterfly Plague* (New York: Viking, 1969), 395.

Chapter Three

1. Patricia Black, "Dangerous Words: An interview with Timothy Findley," *Carousel* 10 (1994): 37.

2. Timothy Findley, *The Wars* (1977; reprint, New York: Penguin, 1978), 9, 182; hereafter cited in text as *Wars*.

3. Frank Davey, "Homoerotic Capitalism: *The Wars*," in *Post-National Arguments: The Politics of the Anglophone-Canadian Novel Since 1967* (Toronto: University of Toronto Press, 1993), 125; hereafter cited in text.

4. Heather Sanderson, "Robert and Taffler: Homosexuality and the Discourse of Gender in Timothy Findley's *The Wars*," *Textual Studies in Canada* 8 (1996): 82–95, and Tom Hastings, "Into the Fire: Masculinities and Militarism in Timothy Findley's *The Wars*."

5. Simone Vauthier, "The Dubious Battle of Storytelling: Narrative Strategies in Timothy Findley's *The Wars*," in *Gaining Ground: European Critics on Canadian Literature,* ed. Robert Kroetsch and Reingard M. Nischik (Edmonton: NeWest, 1985), 16–17; hereafter cited in text.

6. Eve Kosofsky Sedgwick, *Between Men: English Literature and Male Homosocial Desire* (New York: Columbia University Press, 1985), 94–95.

7. Lorraine York, " 'A Shout of Recognition': 'Likeness' and the Art of Simile in Timothy Findley's *The Wars*," *English Studies in Canada* 11, no. 2 (June 1985): 224–25.

8. Walter Benjamin, "Theses on the Philosophy of History," in *Illuminations,* by Walter Benjamin, ed. Hannah Arendt, trans. Harry Zohn. (1968; reprint, New York: Shocken, 1985), 256.

9. Evelyn Cobley, "Postmodernist War Fiction: Findley's *The Wars,*" *Canadian Literature* 147 (Winter 1995): 119; hereafter cited in text.

10. Timothy Findley, *Famous Last Words* (Toronto: Clarke, Irwin, 1981), v; hereafter cited as *Words*.

11. K. K. Ruthven, *A Guide to Ezra Pound's Personae* (Berkeley: University of California Press, 1969), 126; G. S. Fraser, *Ezra Pound* (Glasgow: Oliver, 1962), 62.

12. Martin Kuester, "Timothy Findley's Metafictional Histories," in *Framing Truths: Parodic Structures in Contemporary English-Canadian Historical Novels* (Toronto: University of Toronto Press, 1992), 87; hereafter cited in text.

13. Stephen Scobie, "Eye-Deep in Hell: Ezra Pound, Timothy Findley, and Hugh Selwyn Mauberley," *Essays on Canadian Writing* 30 (Winter 1984–1985), 209.

14. Linda Hutcheon, *A Theory of Parody: The Teachings of Twentieth-Century Art Forms* (New York: Methuen, 1985), 111.

15. David Williams, *Confessional Fictions: A Portrait of the Artist in the Canadian Novel* (Toronto: University of Toronto Press, 1991), 160; hereafter cited in text.

16. Richard Dellamora, "Becoming-Homosexual/Becoming-Canadian: Ironic Voice and the Politics of Location in Timothy Findley's *Famous Last Words*," in *Double-Talking: Essays on Verbal and Visual Ironies in Canadian Contemporary Art and Literature,* ed. Linda Hutcheon (Toronto: ECW, 1992), 181.

17. T. S. Eliot, "The Wasteland," in *T. S. Eliot: Collected Poems 1909–1962* (London: Faber, 1963), 79.

18. Timothy Findley, *The Trials of Ezra Pound* (Winnipeg: Blizzard, 1994), 7; hereafter cited in text as *Trials*.

19. Barbara Gabriel, "Masks and Icons: An Interview with Timothy Findley," *The Canadian Forum* (February 1986): 35.

20. John Xiros Cooper, "Stuck or Mended?" *Canadian Literature* 151 (Winter 1996): 122.

Chapter Four

1. Timothy Findley, *Not Wanted on the Voyage* (New York: Penguin, 1984), 3; hereafter cited in text as *Voyage*.
2. Edward Said, *Beginnings: Intention and Method* (New York: Columbia University Press, 1985), xvii.
3. Helen Tiffin, "*Not Wanted on the Voyage*: Textual Imperialism and Post-colonial Resistance," *Australian-Canadian Studies* 6, no. 2 (1989): 47–56.
4. Donna Palmateer Pennee, *Praying for Rain: Timothy Findley's "Not Wanted on the Voyage"* (Toronto: ECW, 1993).
5. Cecilia Martell, "Unpacking the Baggage: 'Camp' Humour in Timothy Findley's *Not Wanted on the Voyage*," *Canadian Literature* 148 (Spring 1996): 97.
6. Barbara Gabriel, "Performing Theory, Performing Gender: Critical Postscript," *Essays on Canadian Writing* 54 (Winter 1994): 243.
7. George Woodcock, "Timothy Findley's Gnostic Parable," *Canadian Literature* 111 (1986): 236.
8. Mervyn Nicholson, "God, Noah, Lord Byron—and Timothy Findley," *Ariel* 23, no. 2 (April 1992): 87, 88.
9. Diana Brydon, "The Dream of Tory Origins: Inventing Canadian Beginnings," *Australian-Canadian Studies* 6, no. 2 (1989): 35–46.
10. Kenneth D. McRae, "The Structure of Canadian History," in *The Founding of New Societies*, ed. Louis Hartz (New York: Harcourt, Brace & World, 1964), 219–74.
11. George Grant, *Lament for a Nation: The Defeat of Canadian Nationalism* (Toronto: McClelland & Stewart, 1970), 71.
12. Arthur Kroker, *Technology and the Canadian Mind: Innis/McLuhan/Grant* (Montreal: New World Perspectives, 1984), 26.
13. Lorraine York, " 'The Things That Are Seen in the Flashes': Timothy Findley's *Inside Memory* as Photographic Life Writing," *Modern Fiction Studies* 40, no. 3 (Fall 1994): 645.

Chapter Five

1. Timothy Findley, *The Telling of Lies: A Mystery* (New York: Viking Penguin, 1986), 11; hereafter cited in text as *Lies*.
2. For more information on the Cameron case, which lies behind the plot of *The Telling of Lies* and the character of Kurtz in *Headhunter*, see Anne Collins, *In the Sleep Room: The Story of the CIA Brainwashing Experiments in Canada* (Toronto: Lester and Orpen Dennys, 1988); Harvey Weinstein, *A Father, a Son and the CIA* (Toronto: James Lorimer, 1988); and Gordon Thomas, *Journey into Madness: Medical Torture and the Mind Controllers* (New York: Bantam, 1988).

3. Catherine Hunter, "Hiding the Unhidden: The Telling of Stories and *The Telling of Lies,*" *West Coast Line* 24, no. 2 (1990): 106; hereafter cited in text.

4. Anne Geddes Bailey, "Misrepresentations of Vanessa Van Horne: Intertextual Clues in Timothy Findley's *The Telling of Lies,*" *Essays in Canadian Writing* 55 (Spring 1995); hereafter cited in text.

5. Carol Gilligan, *In a Different Voice: Psychological Theory and Women's Development* (1982; reprint, with a new preface by the author, Cambridge, Mass: Harvard University Press, 1993).

6. Jeffrey Canton, "Interview with Timothy Findley," *Paragraph* 15, no. 1 (Summer 1993): 4.

7. Margaret Atwood, afterword to *The Journals of Susanna Moodie* (Toronto: Oxford University Press, 1970), 62.

8. Jay Clayton and Eric Rothstein, "Figures in the Corpus," in *Influence and Intertextuality in Literary History,* ed. Jay Clayton and Eric Rothstein (Madison: University of Wisconsin Press, 1991), 20.

Chapter Six

1. Timothy Findley, *Can You See Me Yet?* (Vancouver: Talonbooks, 1977), 42; hereafter cited in text as *Yet.*

2. Timothy Findley, *The Piano Man's Daughter* (Toronto: Harper-Collins, 1995), 339; hereafter cited in text as *Daughter.*

3. Philip Marchand, "Findley Weaves Gothic Romance," *Toronto Star,* 22 April 1995, H16; hereafter cited in text.

4. John Hulcoop, "Findley's Eighth," *Canadian Literature* 151 (Winter 1996): 171.

5. Timothy Findley, *You Went Away* (Toronto: HarperCollins, 1996), 1; hereafter cited in text as *Away.*

6. Harry Lane, " 'Not His own Person': Questions of Betrayal in *The Stillborn Lover,*" *Queen's Quarterly* 100, no. 2 (Summer 1993): 442.

7. Timothy Findley, *The Stillborn Lover* (Winnipeg: Blizzard, 1993), 90; hereafter cited in text as *Lover.*

8. Michel Foucault, *The History of Sexuality: Volume 1: An Introduction,* trans. Robert Hurley (1978; reprint, New York: Vintage, 1990), 45.

Selected Bibliography

PRIMARY SOURCES

Novels

The Last of the Crazy People. London: Macdonald,1967; Toronto: Macmillan, 1977.
The Butterfly Plague. New York: Viking, 1969. Rev. ed. Markham, Ont.: Penguin, 1986.
The Wars. Toronto: Clarke, Irwin: 1977; Markham, Ont.: Penguin, 1986.
Famous Last Words. Toronto: Clarke, Irwin, 1981.
Not Wanted on the Voyage. Markham, Ont.: Viking, 1984.
The Telling of Lies: A Mystery. Markham, Ont.: Viking, 1986.
Headhunter. Toronto: HarperCollins, 1993.
The Piano Man's Daughter. Toronto: HarperCollins, 1995.
You Went Away. Toronto: HarperCollins, 1996.

Short Story Collections

Dinner along the Amazon. Markham, Ont.: Penguin, 1984.
Stones. Markham, Ont.: Penguin, 1988.
Dust to Dust: Stories. Toronto: HarperCollins, 1997.

Plays

Can You See Me Yet? Talonbooks: 1977.
The Paper People. Canadian Drama 9, no. 1 (1983): 62–164.
The Journey: A Montage for Radio. Canadian Drama 10, no. 1 (1984): 116–40.
The Stillborn Lover. Winnipeg: Blizzard, 1993.
The Trials of Ezra Pound. Winnipeg: Blizzard, 1994.

Memoirs

"Legends." *Landfall* 40, no. 3 (September 1986): 327–32.
"My Final Hour." *Journal of Canadian Studies* 22, no. 1 (Spring 1987): 5–16.
Inside Memory: Pages from a Writer's Workbook. Toronto: HarperCollins, 1990.
"Significant Others." *Journal of Canadian Studies/Revue d'etudes canadiennes* 28, no. 4 (Winter 1993–1994): 149–59.

Critical Commentary

Afterword to *The Diviners,* by Margaret Laurence. Toronto: McClelland & Stewart, 1984.

"Alice Drops Her Cigarette on the Floor . . . (William Whitehead looking over Timothy Findley's Shoulder)." *Canadian Literature* 91 (Winter 1981): 10–21.

Interviews

Aitken, Johan. " 'Long Live the Dead': An Interview with Timothy Findley." *Journal of Canadian Fiction* 33 (1982): 79–93.
Black, Patricia. "Dangerous Words: An Interview with Timothy Findley." *Carousel* 10 (1994): 25–44.
Cameron, Donald. "Timothy Findley: 'Make Peace with Nature, Now.' " In *Conversations with Canadian Novelists*, 1:49–63. Toronto: Macmillan, 1973.
Canton, Jeffrey. "Interview with Timothy Findley."*Paragraph* 15, no. 1 (Summer 1993): 3–7.
Gabriel, Barbara. "Masks and Icons: An Interview with Timothy Findley." *The Canadian Forum* (February 1986): 31–36.
Gibson, Graeme. "Timothy Findley." In *Eleven Canadian Novelists*, 115–50. Toronto: Anansi, 1973.
Kruk, Laurie. "I Want Edge: An Interview with Timothy Findley." *Canadian Literature* 148 (Spring 1996): 115–29.
Meyer, Bruce and Brian O'Riordan. "Timothy Findley: *The Marvel of Reality*." In *In Their Words: Interviews with Fourteen Canadian Writers*, 44–55. Toronto: Anansi, 1984.
Montador, Gordon. "Talking with Tiff." *The Body Politic* (October 1984): 27–30.
Summers, Alison. "Interview with Timothy Findley." *Canadian Literature* 91 (Winter 1981): 49–57.

SECONDARY SOURCES

Bibliographies

Roberts, Carol and Lynne Macdonald. *Timothy Findley: An Annotated Bibliography*. Toronto: ECW, 1990. Lists all of Findley's writing (books, play productions, films, audiovisual materials, manuscripts, and contributions to periodicals and books). Annotates all works on Timothy Findley (articles and sections of books, theses, and awards) and selected reviews of his work up to 1988.

Biographies

Roberts, Carol. "The Perfection of Gesture: Timothy Findley and Canadian Theatre." *Theatre History in Canada* 21, no. 1 (1991): 22–36. Describes Findley's career as an actor, playwright, and writer for radio and television, and argues that this theatrical work has influenced his other writing.

————. *Timothy Findley: Stories from a Life.* Toronto: ECW, 1994. A thorough and sympathetic story of Findley's life to 1993.

Books and Parts of Books

Brydon, Diana. *Writing on Trial: Timothy Findley's 'Famous Last Words.'* Toronto: ECW, 1995. A reading of *Famous Last Words* as a staging and mediating of debates around the appeal and horrors of fascism as a cultural, aesthetic, and political movement that has survived the defeat of the Nazis.

————. "Timothy Findley: A Post-Holocaust, Post-Colonial Vision." In *International Literature in English: Essays on the Major Writers,* ed. Robert L. Ross, 583–92. New York: Garland, 1991. Argues that Findley's work addresses the issues raised by the holocaust and decolonization, two of the central events of the twentieth century.

————. " 'Rogues and Brutes . . . in Pinstripe Suits': Timothy Findley's *Headhunter.*" In *Imperialism and Gender: Constructions of Masculinity,* ed. C. E. Gittings, 192–99. London: Dangaroo, 1996. A reading of *Headhunter*'s critique of capitalist models of masculinity through the novel's recycling of Conrad's *Heart of Darkness* in a futuristic Canadian setting.

Davey, Frank. "Homoerotic Capitalism: *The Wars.*" In *Post-National Arguments: The Politics of the Anglophone-Canadian Novel Since 1967,* 113–27. Toronto: University of Toronto Press, 1993. A controversial reading of *The Wars* as a postnationalist text.

Dellamora, Richard. "Becoming-Homosexual/Becoming-Canadian: Ironic Voice and the Politics of Location in Timothy Findley's *Famous Last Words.*" In *Double-Talking: Essays on Verbal and Visual Ironies in Contemporary Canadian Art and Literature,* ed. Linda Hutcheon, 172–200. Toronto: ECW, 1992. A thought-provoking and innovative reading of the sexual politics of location in *Famous Last Words* that is relevant to an understanding of all of Findley's work.

Gittings, Christopher E. " 'What Are Soldiers For?': Re-making Masculinities in Timothy Findley's *The Wars.*" In *Imperialism and Gender: Constructions of Masculinity,* ed. C. E. Gittings, 186–91. London: Dangaroo, 1996. A careful study of *The Wars'* critique of models for masculinity employing the insights of postcolonial and queer theorists.

Hulcoop, John F. "Timothy Findley." In *Canadian Writers Since 1960.* Vol. 53 of *Dictionary of Literary Biography,* ed. W. H. New, 181–91. Detroit: Gale, 1986. A valuable survey of Findley's life and work.

Kuester, Martin. "Timothy Findley's Metafictional Histories: Modernist Parodies or Parodies of Modernism?" In *Framing Truths: Parodic Structures in Contemporary English-Canadian Historical Novels,* 52–94. Toronto: University of Toronto Press, 1992. A thorough reading of *The Wars* and *Famous Last Words* as parodic texts within a predominantly modernist tradition.

Pennee, Donna Palmateer. *Moral Metafiction: Counter-discourse in the Novels of Timothy Findley.* Toronto: ECW, 1991. A study of Findley's work to *The Telling of Lies* as ethical metafiction.

————. *Praying for Rain: Timothy Findley's "Not Wanted on the Voyage."* Toronto: ECW, 1993. A thorough reading of *Not Wanted on the Voyage* as revisionist fiction.

Ricou, Laurie. "Obscured by Violence: Timothy Findley's *The Wars.*" In *Violence in the Canadian Novel since 1960*, edited by Virginia Harger-Grinling and Terry Goldie, 125–37. St. John's, Newfoundland: Memorial University, 1981. An important early article on violence in *The Wars.*

Seddon, Elizabeth. "The Reader as Actor in the Novels of Timothy Findley." In *Future Indicative: Literary Theory and Canadian Literature*, edited by John Moss, 213–30. Ottawa: University of Ottawa Press, 1987. Uses reader response theory to illuminate *The Butterfly Plague, The Wars,* and *Famous Last Words.*

Vauthier, Simone. "The Dubious Battle of Storytelling: Narrative Strategies in Timothy Findley's *The Wars.*" In *Gaining Ground: European Critics on Canadian Literature*, edited by Robert Kroetsch and Reingard M. Nischik, 11–39. Edmonton: NeWest, 1985: 11–39. The most thorough analysis from a narratological perspective of narrative strategies in *The Wars.*

Williams, David. "The Aesthete's Reply: 'A Prose Kinema' in *Famous Last Words.*" In *Confessional Fictions: A Portrait of the Artist in the Canadian Novel*, 237–62. Toronto: University of Toronto Press, 1991. Challenges the dominant view of *Famous Last Words* as postmodernist, locating instead its indebtedness to late-nineteenth-century aestheticism.

York, Lorraine M. 'Violent Stillness': Timothy Findley's Use of Photography." In *The Other Side of Dailiness: Photography in the Works of Alice Munro, Timothy Findley, Michael Ondaatje, and Margaret Laurence*, 51–92. Toronto: ECW, 1988. A wide-ranging study of the changing role of photography in Findley's work, affirming its increasingly humanist function, and concluding with *Not Wanted on the Voyage.*

————. *Introducing Timothy Findley's "The Wars."* Toronto: ECW, 1990. An introduction to *The Wars* as a canonical text in the Canadian literary tradition.

————. *Front Lines: The Fiction of Timothy Findley.* Toronto: ECW, 1991. Reads Findley's work through its focus on war as actuality and metaphor.

Articles

Bailey, Anne Geddes. "Misrepresentations of Vanessa Van Horne: Intertextual Clues in Timothy Findley's *The Telling of Lies*" *Essays in Canadian Writing* 55 (Spring 1995): 191–213. Argues that *The Telling of Lies,* through its

deployment of an unreliable narrator, is more problematic morally than
critics have assumed.

Benson, Eugene. "Whispers of Chaos: Famous Last Words." *World Literature
Written in English* 21 (1982): 599–606. A discussion of the centrality of
violence in Findley's work.

Brydon, Diana. "A Devotion to Fragility: Timothy Findley's *The Wars*." *World
Literature Written in English* 26, no. 1. (1986): 75–84. Examines the
interplay of violence and beauty in the aesthetic of *The Wars*.

———. " 'It Could Not Be Told': Making Meaning in Timothy Findley's *The
Wars*." *Journal of Commonwealth Literature* 21 (1986): 62–79. Discusses
how *The Wars* employs the trope of the unspeakable.

———. "The Dream of Tory Origins: Inventing Canadian Beginnings."
Australian-Canadian Studies 6, no. 2 (1989): 35–46. Situates *Not Wanted
on the Voyage* within the Canadian cultural tradition of lamenting the
passing of the Tory dream.

Cobley, Evelyn. "Postmodernist War Fiction: Findley's *The Wars*." *Canadian Literature* 147 (Winter 1995): 98–126. A thorough placing of *The Wars*
within the context of the genre of twentieth-century war fiction.

Dopp, Jamie. "Reading as Collaboration in Timothy Findley's *Famous Last
Words*." *Studies in Canadian Literature* 20, no. 1 (1995): 1–15. An examination of the complicit and enabling dimensions of how reading is constructed as a collaborative act in *Famous Last Words*.

Duffy, Dennis. "Let Us Compare Histories: Meaning and Mythology in Findley's
Famous Last Words." *Essays on Canadian Writing* 30 (Winter 1984–1985):
187–205. Analyzes the interplay of history and mythology in *Famous
Last Words*.

———. "The Rejection of Modernity in Recent Canadian Fiction." *Canadian
Issues/Themes canadiens* 7 (1985): 260–73. Expresses dissatisfaction with
The Wars as a rejection of modern culture.

Gabriel, Barbara. "Staging Montrosity: Genre, Life-Writing, and Timothy
Findley's *The Last of the Crazy People*." *Essays on Canadian Writing* 54
(Winter 1994): 168–97. A groundbreaking reading of *The Last of the
Crazy People* from the perspective of contemporary gender and perfor-
mance theories.

Gardner, David and Timothy Findley. "On *The Paper People*." *Canadian Drama* 9,
no. 1 (1983): 60–61. Discusses themes and techniques in *The Paper
People*.

Howells, Coral Ann. " 'History as She is Never Writ': *The Wars* and *Famous Last
Words*." *Kunapipi* 6, no. 1 (1984): 49–56. Reads these texts as historical
novels that self-consciously foreground the acts of reading and writing.

———. " ''Tis Sixty Years Since': Timothy Findley's *The Wars* and Roger
McDonald's *1915*." *World Literature Written in English* 23 (Winter 1984):
129–36. Situates comparative readings of these texts in the tradition of
fiction of the First World War.

Hulcoop, John F. "Look! Listen! Mark My Words! Paying Attention to Timothy Findley's Fiction." *Canadian Literature* 91 (1981): 22–47. An important early article focusing on style and the importance of paying attention in Findley's fictional world.

Hunter, Catherine. "Hiding the Unhidden: The Telling of Stories and *The Telling of Lies*." *West Coast Line* 24, no. 2 (1990): 99–108. An excellent analysis of the use and questioning of the generic conventions of the mystery and detective novel in *The Telling of Lies*.

Hutcheon, Linda. "Canadian Historiographic Metafiction." *Essays on Canadian Writing* 30 (Winter 1984–1985): 228–38. Revised as "Historigraphic Metafiction" in *The Canadian Postmodern: A Study of Contemporary English-Canadian Fiction*. (Toronto: Oxford University Press, 1988), 61–77. Stresses the importance of the reader as voyeur and link between fact and fiction in the genre of historiographic metafiction, which she identifies as the mode of *Famous Last Words*.

Ingham, David. "Bashing the Fascists: The Moral Dimensions of Findley's Fiction." *Studies in Canadian Literature* 15, no.2 (1990): 33–54. Focuses on ethics and the fascist theme in *Famous Last Words*.

Irvine, Lorna. "Crises of the Legitimate: Matt Cohen and Timothy Findley." *The American Review of Canadian Studies* 19 (Spring 1989): 15–23. In her focus on *The Telling of Lies*, Irvine details why she finds the work feminist.

Klovan, Peter. " 'Bright and Good': Timothy Findley's *The Wars*." *Canadian Literature* 91 (1981): 58–69. An early discussion of themes in *The Wars* arguing that Robert's journey is tragic, in that he transcends the elemental forces that defeat him.

Kroller, Eva Marie. "The Exploding Frame: Uses of Photography in Timothy Findley's *The Wars*." *Journal of Canadian Studies/Revue d'etudes canadiennes* 16, nos. 3–4 (Fall–Winter 1981): 68–74. Stresses the ambiguity and postmodernist function of photography in *The Wars*.

———. "The Eye in the Text: Timothy Findley's *The Last of the Crazy People* and Alice Munro's *Lives of Girls and Women*. *World Literature Written in English* 25, no. 2 (Spring 1984): 366–74. Reads these texts as metafiction, focusing on the perceptions of the young protagonists.

Lane, Harry. " 'Not his own person': Questions of Betrayal in *The Stillborn Lover*." *Queen's Quarterly* 100, no. 2 (Summer 1993): 441–56. A thoroughly researched and wide-ranging discussion of the text and first production of this play.

McKenzie, Sister M. L. "Memories of the Great War: Graves, Sassoon, and Findley." *University of Toronto Quarterly* 55, no. 4 (Summer 1986): 395–411. Situates *The Wars* within the context of British fiction of the First World War.

Marshall, Brenda. "Meta(Hi)Story: *Timothy Findley's 'Famous Last Words.'* " *The International Fiction Review* 16, no. 1 (1989): 17–22. Focuses on the metafictional and postmodernist dimensions of *Famous Last Words*.

Martell, Cecilia. "Unpacking the Baggage: 'Camp' Humour in Timothy Find-
    ley's *Not Wanted on the Voyage*," *Canadian Literature* 148 (Spring 1996):
    96–111. The first discussion of camp humour in this novel.
Miller, Mary Jane. "An Analysis of *The Paper People*." *Canadian Drama* 9, no. 1.
    (1983): 49–59. An appreciative reading of the themes and structure of
    The Paper People.
Murray, Don. "Seeing and Surviving in Timothy Findley's Short Stories." *Studies
    in Canadian Literature* 13 (1988): 200–22. A thematic reading of the
    short stories.
Nicholson, Mervyn. "God, Noah, Lord Byron—and Timothy Findley." *Ariel*
    23, no. 2 (April 1992): 87–107. Argues that *Not Wanted on the Voyage* is
    part of a tradition of revisionary readings of biblical narratives begun in
    the Romantic period.
Pirie, Bruce. "The Dragon in the Fog: 'Displaced Mythology' in *The Wars*."
    Canadian Literature 91 (Winter 1981): 70–79. Discusses *The Wars* as a
    quest narrative.
Sanderson, Heather. "Robert and Taffler: Homosexuality and the Discourse of
    Gender in Timothy Findley's *The Wars*." *Textual Studies in Canada* 8
    (1996): 82–95. Uses the insights of contemporary gender and queer the-
    ory to provide a more detailed analysis of this dimension of *The Wars* than
    has yet been made.
Scobie, Stephen. "Eye-Deep in Hell: Ezra Pound, Timothy Findley, and Hugh
    Selwyn Mauberley." *Essays on Canadian Writing* 30 (Winter 1984–1985):
    206–27. Examines the use of Pound's person and poem as characters in
    Famous Last Words.
————. "I and I: Phyllis Webb's 'I Daniel.' " *Open Letter* 6, nos. 2–3 (Summer–Fall
    1985): 61–70. Discusses Webb's poem as an intertextual double to
    Famous Last Words, analyzing the novel's mirror imagery, use of Pound's
    Mauberley, and references to the biblical Book of Daniel.
Shields, E. F. "Mauberley's Lies: Fact and Fiction in Timothy Findley's *Famous
    Last Words*." *Journal of Canadian Studies* 22, no. 4 (1987–1988): 44–59.
    Differentiates between the facts and fictions that *Famous Last Words* con-
    fuses. A very useful source for the historical underpinnings of this novel.
————. " 'The Perfect Voice': Mauberley as Narrator in Timothy Findley's
    Famous Last Words." *Canadian Literature* 119 (1988): 84–98. A positive
    assessment of Findley's use of Mauberley as a narrator in *Famous Last
    Words*.
Tiffin, Helen M. "*Not Wanted on the Voyage*: Textual Imperialism and Post-colonial
    Resistance." *Australian-Canadian Studies* 6, no. 2 (1989): 47–56. Revised
    as "Radical Otherness and Hybridity: Timothy Findley's *Not Wanted on
    the Voyage*" in Bill Ashcroft, Gareth Giffiths, and Helen Tiffin, *The Empire
    Writes Back: Theory and Practice in Post-Colonial Literature* (New York:
    Routledge, 1989), 97–104. A postcolonial reading of *Not Wanted on the
    Voyage*.

Walton, Priscilla. " 'This isn't a fairy tale. . . . It's mythology': The Colonial Perspective in *Famous Last Words*." *Commonwealth* 14, no. 1 (Autumn 1991): 9–15. A postcolonial reading of *Famous Last Words*.

Woodcock, George. Timothy Findley's Gnostic Parable." *Canadian Literature* 111 (1986): 232–37. Argues that *Not Wanted on the Voyage* is consistent with Gnostic readings of the Bible.

York, Lorraine M. " 'A Shout of Recognition': 'Likeness' and the Art of Simile in Timothy Findley's *The Wars*." *English Studies in Canada* 11, no. 2 (June 1985): 223–30. Discusses the function of Findley's use of similes linking war and civilian life in *The Wars*.

————. " 'The Things That Are Seen in the Flashes': Timothy Findley's *Inside Memory* as Photographic Life Writing. *Modern Fiction Studies* 40, no. 3 (Fall 1994): 643–56. Analyzes *Inside Memory* as an example of photographic life writing and a subversive mix of genres that proceeds through epiphany.

Reviews

Cooper, John Xiros. "Stuck or Mended?" Review of *The Trials of Ezra Pound*. *Canadian Literature* 151 (Winter 1996): 121–23. A glowing review that sees the play as sophisticated commentary on modernism's strengths and failings.

Hulcoop, John F. "Findley's Eighth." Review of *The Piano Man's Daughter*. *Canadian Literature* 151 (Winter 1996): 169–71. The disappointed review of a Findley devotee, who finds the switch to the "romantic pastoral" mode in *The Piano Man's Daughter* unsatisfying.

Marchand, Philip. "Findley Weaves Gothic Romance." Review of *The Piano Man's Daughter*. *The Toronto Star*, 22 April 1995, H16. A mixed assessment of *Daughter*'s strengths and weaknesses, stressing its tone, form, and incorporation of Findley's fondness for the elegiac mode.

Index

The Author

Diana Brydon is professor of English at the University of Guelph, where she teaches Canadian literature and postcolonial literatures and theory. She was educated at the University of Toronto and the Australian National University, and has taught at the Universities of Toronto, Adelaide, and British Columbia, as well as briefly in Brazil.

She has published *Christina Stead* (London and New York: Macmillan and Barnes Noble, 1987), *Writing on Trial: Timothy Findley's Famous Last Words* (Toronto: ECW, 1995) and, with Helen Tiffin, *Decolonising Fictions* (London: Dangaroo, 1993). She is guest editor of the postcolonial special issue of *Essays on Canadian Writing* (1995) and has published extensively on postcolonial literatures, criticism, and theory. Her next project involves investigating the interdisciplinary history of the critical concept of postcolonialism.

The Editor

Robert Lecker is professor of English at McGill University in Montreal. He received his Ph.D. from York University. Professor Lecker is the author of numerous critical studies, including *On the Line* (1982), *Robert Kroetch* (1986), *An Other I* (1988), and *Making It Real: The Canonization of English-Canadian Literature* (1995). He is the editor of the critical journal *Essays on Canadian Writing* and of many collections of critical essays, the most recent of which is *Canadian Canons: Essays in Literary Value* (1991). He is the founding and current general editor of Twayne's Masterwork Studies, and the editor of the Twayne World Authors Series on Canadian writers. He is also the general editor of G. K. Hall's Critical Essays on World Literature series.